Serendipitous Outings

Near New York City

Help Us Keep This Guide Up to Date

Every effort has been made by the authors and editors to make this guide as accurate and useful as possible. However, many changes can occur after a guide is published—establishments close, phone numbers change, hiking trails are rerouted, facilities come under new management, etc.

We would love to hear from you concerning your experiences with this guide and how you feel it could be improved and be kept up to date. While we may not be able to respond to all comments and suggestions, we'll take them to heart, and we'll make certain to share them with the authors. Please send your comments and suggestions to the following address:

The Globe Pequot Press
Reader Response/Editorial Department
P.O. Box 480
Guilford, CT 06437

Or you may e-mail us at:

editorial@GlobePequot.com

Thanks for your input, and happy travels!

Serendipitous Outings

Near New York City

On Foot in New Jersey,
Long Island, the Hudson Valley,
Connecticut, and Pennsylvania

MARINA HARRISON AND LUCY D. ROSENFELD
ILLUSTRATIONS BY LUCY D. ROSENFELD

INSIDERS' GUIDE®

GUILFORD, CONNECTICUT
AN IMPRINT OF THE GLOBE PEQUOT PRESS

Although thorough efforts have been made to verify hours of operation and admission charges and rates, these items often change at the whim of proprietors or as a result of governmental budgets. Therefore, call ahead for current information before traveling.

Maps provided are for reference only and should be used in conjunction with a road map. Distances suggested are approximate.

To buy books in quantity for corporate use or incentives, call **(800) 962–0973, ext. 4551,** or e-mail **premiums@GlobePequot.com.**

INSIDERS' GUIDE®

Illustrations by Lucy D. Rosenfeld
Text design by Gina Grasso

Library of Congress Cataloging-in-Publication Data

Harrison, Marina, 1939–
    Serendipitous outings near New York City : interesting strolls in New Jersey, Long Island, the Hudson Valley, Connecticut, and Pennsylvania / Marina Harrison and Lucy D. Rosenfeld; illustrations by Lucy D. Rosenfeld.— 1st Globe Pequot ed.
        p: cm.
    Includes bibliographical references and index.
    ISBN–13: 978–0–7627–3668–3
    ISBN–10: 0-7627-3668-2
    1. New York Region—Guidebooks. 2. Walking—New York Region—Guidebooks.
3. Middle Atlantic States—Guidebooks. 4. Walking—Middle Atlantic States—Guidebooks.
5. Bird watching—New York Region—Guidebooks. I. Rosenfeld, Lucy D., 1939– II. Title.
    F128.18.H357 2006
    917.404'44—dc22
                                                                2005036381

Manufactured in the United States of America
First Globe Pequot Edition/First Printing

Contents

Serendipitous Outings

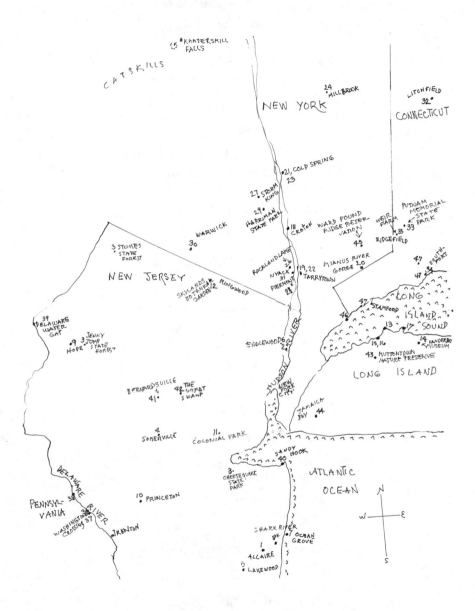

The Hudson Valley (West)

Bird-Watching

Preface

This is a book of outings for walkers of every description. We hope that experienced trail hikers, antique-village enthusiasts, nature lovers, adventuresome wanderers, bird watchers, and leisure-time strollers who enjoy conversation, peace, and quiet will all find walks to their taste in this book. To this end we have compiled a list of outings that includes some of the oddest and prettiest locations, as well as the more traditional natural park sites. All of our walks are well within the abilities of the average family, and some are even easier. A few are for the more rugged hikers, but the views and scenery make them well worth the effort. You'll find outings especially designated for the physically challenged and others for people with particular interests: herbs, gravestones, mushrooms, apple picking, fine art, physical fitness, and beachcombing, among them.

In no way do we pretend that this is a comprehensive guide to all the walks in the New York City area. And obviously there are many books dedicated to specific interests. What we have tried to do is to offer a collection of outings that will pique the fancy and appeal to many different tastes.

Despite the massive overbuilding of this region, there still are many lovely places to explore. Over a five-year period we have crisscrossed our area, from Long Island to Westchester and Putnam, from New Jersey's seashore to its interior canals, from Connecticut's coast to its colonial villages. We have looked for bird-watching sites along the way, and you'll find those we have chosen make for fine walking as well as birding. Our village walking tours are through communities that have managed to retain an architectural identity despite growth and inroads of the twentieth century. Each will bring you the aura of a special time or place: a Moravian stone village, a Hudson River landing, a Connecticut colonial town, a Victorian Methodist camp-village.

While researching these sites we have been encouraged by the sense of preservation that has swept the area. New parklands, gifts of unspoiled greenery, and careful conservation of old houses and antique buildings are everywhere. Within a few dozen miles of the city you'll find wonderful, restorative scenery and many uncrowded trails and pathways.

Each of our outings suggests the best time for a hike in the region—and they are not all in the spring! Fall foliage and winter snow walks are included, as are beach and lakeside strolls. We also advise you when not to walk in some areas; we prefer uncrowded and solitary strolls, and we assume you do, too. We also note the difficulty of each hike and designate certain trips as especially good for small children, for those in wheelchairs, and for the elderly. You'll find information on parking fees, availability of food and drink, maps, and what to take along (comfortable shoes!), as well as major historic sites and other more touristy things to do after your walk.

The routes we have suggested are generally the shortest; however, in some cases we have avoided congested areas by recommending slightly longer, but more pleasant, approaches.

We wish you many pleasant days of walking, as we have had, and perhaps the addition to your city life of some new country-ish delights. We hope that in most cases you can take your children along on these outings and can show them that a world of serene beauty and of wide-ranging interests awaits them outside the urban scene. And if you're familiar with other nearby special locales that we have missed, please let us know!

New Jersey

01 | A "Deserted" Village

Allaire State Park

This picturesque spot in Monmouth County was once a bustling iron forge center, known in 1763 as the Williamsburg Forge. By 1822 one Benjamin Howell had joined with a brass founder named James P. Allaire to establish the Howell Works on the site. The village then had 400 people working in bog iron production. (Bog iron ore was produced by decaying vegetation.) The iron was smelted and cast into cauldrons, pots, pipes, stoves, and other objects.

By the mid-nineteenth century, however, higher-grade iron ore in western areas began to drive the forge out of business. Soon Allaire Village lost its manufacturing base, and eventually the entire site was abandoned.

What we see as we walk through today is a charming small village, totally uninhabited except for a park ranger station and a general store. The restoration of the old buildings has been careful, not at all "hokey." Strolling through the village, with its widely separated buildings, is historically interesting and quite picturesque. The roadway winds through what's left of the village— about twenty buildings—from the old Christ Church (a charming white New England–style meetinghouse), past the 1835 bakery, the sawmill, the furnace stack, over little bridges,

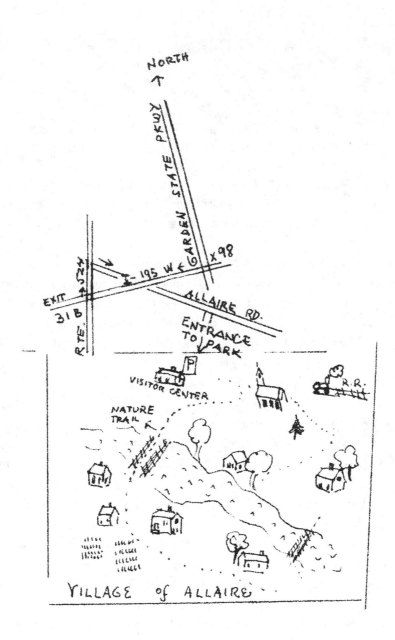

NORTH

GARDEN STATE PKWY

X 98

I-195 W

RTE. 524

EXIT 31 B

R TE.

ALLAIRE RD.

ENTRANCE TO PARK

VISITOR CENTER

R.R.

NATURE TRAIL

VILLAGE of ALLAIRE

across fields, and into the woods. In addition to the village, there are several nice nature trails. The entire environment re-creates the ambiance of a small rural village surrounded by woods and meadows. Its emptiness and lack of cars, noise, or smoke make it curiously still. And the gentle sloping hillsides with brooks rippling by provide very pleasant country strolling.

The village itself is a small part of a state park. There are trails, camping, and other facilities in the park. A small fee is charged for parking. The park is open officially from Memorial Day to Labor Day, but you can walk through the village at any time except during January and February. There are tours and other conveniences, such as food, restrooms, and exhibits, as well as a steam train ride on the Pine Creek Railroad available every day in season and on weekends (except in winter).

If you are taking children along, we recommend visiting the village when many of the facilities are open, for there is a vari-ety of events, such as cider making, fishing contests for chil-dren, and candle dipping, as well as that steam train ride. Among other events are art shows, concerts, and formal exhibits of quilts, tools, and antique clothing. Call (732) 938–2253 for more information.

If, however, you prefer a quieter time or are a walker seeking solitude and natural beauty, visit Allaire out of season; it can get crowded on summer weekends. We visited both in spring and fall and found it truly a deserted village, in every sense.

The village is open from 10:00 A.M. to 5:00 P.M. Wednesday through Sunday, in season. There is a charge for visiting most buildings; grounds are free. We hasten to add that "open" does not mean that people are parading around in costumes or pro-viding expensive carriage rides for professional photographers. This is a deserted village in the best sense.

If you wish to leave the village and go off onto the wooded trails (much as Allaire's nineteenth-century citizens must have gone into the nearby forest to find a rabbit for supper), you should bring sturdy wet-shoes. The woods surrounding the village are fairly moist underfoot, particularly in spring. You can bring a picnic—there are tables next to the parking area—or in season you can buy refreshments at the visitor center.

The Walk

Though guided tours are available, we liked the self-guided tour, so we could linger as long as we wanted at what we felt were the most interesting spots. You will leave your car at the parking area, and set off, guide map in hand, to your right. There are some twenty buildings—or remains thereof—to be visited, and you can divert your route to the Manasquam Floodplain Trail into the woods, a very pretty nature walk.

Your first stop will be the homes built by Mr. Allaire around 1832, which now house exhibits and information. You can get a map there. The next building is the foreman's cottage, dating to 1827. Farther along you'll find the entrance to the nature trail, at the bridge over the brook, and the site of the original sawmill. In the grinding mill and screw factory, which employed children of the community, the iron objects were ground and polished. The gristmill and blacksmith shop from the 1830s are definitely worth a good look, and so is the old bakery, the upstairs of which served as the schoolroom. (James Allaire provided schooling out of his own pocket.) One of the oldest buildings is the manager's home, which was built about 1798 for the stagecoach driver. You'll next come to the Village General Store, which is still in operation and filled with goodies of many kinds. The carpenter shop and enameling building are next along the walk; the exhibits of antique crafts are held in the enameling building.

Soon you'll reach the furnace stack, the most important of Allaire's historic sites, for this is the last of the state's early iron furnaces. It was powered by a waterwheel; today only the stack remains. The dormitory for the workers is one of the original buildings near the furnace. Mr. Allaire himself lived here, as did many workers. The carriage house, hay barn, and cattle barns are next on the route. Finally, you will come to the charming Christ Church, an Episcopalian church dating from the 1830s. There are foundations and remains of other buildings at Allaire, and the interested walker can delve much more deeply into the past of this quintessentially American village by visiting the library and the exhibits.

After the Walk

Allaire is close to the Atlantic Ocean. In fact, two of the nicest towns on the coast are a short distance away. Spring Lake, probably the prettiest of the shore communities, is just a few miles east of Allaire on Route 524. In this unspoiled turn-of-the-twentieth-century town, be sure to see the octagonal Portuguese Pavilion (at 207 Atlantic Avenue), the Missouri State Building (411 Ocean Road), the Atlas Home (410 Passaic Avenue), the Osborn Farmhouse dating from 1840 (412 Sussex Avenue), Monmouth House Hotel, Warren Hotel, Essex-Sussex Hotel, the railroad station, and the charming rustic bridges across Spring Lake itself. You might wish to see the sights via trolley, which leaves Monday through Friday from Third and Morris Avenues on the hour and half hour, from 10:00 A.M. to 3:30 P.M. The inexpensive thirty-minute ride is picturesque and fun.

Another town to visit, Ocean Grove, a Victorian village founded by Methodists, is described in Outing 07.

02 | A Shore Path below the Palisades
Englewood Cliffs

The towering, majestic cliffs of the Palisades are among the great natural wonders of our region. Situated on the west bank of the Hudson, directly across from upper Manhattan, the Bronx, and Westchester County, they extend for about 40 miles north along the New Jersey and New York shorelines. These formations were named "palisades" because their impressive rampartlike structure reminded the early settlers of a palisade enclosure. In the nineteenth century the rock of the Palisades was quarried to such an extent as to threaten their very existence. Fortunately, the Palisades Interstate Park Commission was formed in 1900, just in time to preserve this precious natural wonder. As you drive across the George Washington Bridge and catch your first glimpse of the dramatic and wondrous cliffs, you're thankful they still exist.

The Shore Path below the Palisades is one of two main walks here, the other being the Long Path, on top. Although both provide wonderful river views and great walking, we especially like the Shore Path. You are always close to the river and feel a certain intimacy with your surroundings; there is a wonderful variety in the terrain along the shore (including a long, slender waterfall); and the views of the cliffs are spectacular from below. But what makes this walk so special is your feeling of being in an isolated spot, far from the congestion of the city, when in fact you are so close. As you walk along, you hear sounds of the gently lapping water and the wind blowing through the trees, and only an occasional motorboat making its way up or down the river. The Shore Path is pleasantly shaded all the way, with dense woodlands of oak and maple that turn strikingly brilliant in the fall.

The trail begins near the George Washington Bridge and continues some 10 miles or so north to the New York State line passing enroute the intriguing stone ruins of a 1930s roofless bathhouse. However, we suggest you concentrate on the section between the Englewood Boat Basin and the Alpine Boat Basin (starting at either place), about 5 miles in all. If energy level and time are not a problem, you might want to do the entire distance, ideally arranging to be met by car at the other end. If you start at the Alpine Boat Basin, you will only have to walk about 1.5 miles before reaching the scenic waterfall, so a walk there and back might be another option. The going is fairly easy and mostly flat, except for a few stone stairs near the Alpine Boat Basin.

Although the trail is never crowded (you might meet an occasional Boy Scout troop or a solitary walker or two), we suggest you go off-season rather than during the summer, when the parking lots in both basins are noisy and crowded. You might want to take along a pair of binoculars to view the river life (occasional waterfowl and other birds) or the shoreline across the river and the more distant Manhattan skyline.

The Walk

Park your car at the Englewood Boat Basin, preferably at the northern end of the second of two extensive parking areas, past playgrounds, picnic areas, and fishing docks. In front of you, next to a gigantic boulder at river's edge, is the Shore Path heading north. Though its white markers are somewhat sporadic, it has been well trod and is clearly delineated all the way.

The path's surface, at first sandy, becomes progressively grassy, then somewhat rocky, then woodsy. While the footing is varied— but mostly flat and easy—because of its irregular surface, you are not likely to see bikers or joggers. Truly, this is a peaceful, reflective walk. As you go north, you pass a stretch that was once a settlement of small farms, quarries, and fishing shacks before the parkland was created. You'll see the curious remains of a cemetery, romantically situated amid a pretty meadow. The winding path, always shaded and pleasant, skirts the river, at times so close you can touch the water. You walk past small beaches and docks and rocky lookout points. Trees grow down to the riverbank, and honeysuckle, grapevines, tall grasses, and shrubs of wild berries adorn the way. Stone picnic tables assembled from the fallen rock and resembling prehistoric formations are found here and there.

After some 3 miles you reach the picturesque Greenbrook Falls, amid a heavily wooded setting. The path then becomes somewhat steeper (although still easy for most walkers), with occasional stone steps up and down past the washouts on the river's edge. We found this part of the walk particularly appealing, with its variety of vegetation and terrain. After another mile or so (about 5.5 miles from the Englewood Boat Basin), you arrive at the Alpine Boat Basin, where there are more parking areas, fishing docks, picnic tables, a refreshment stand (in season), and restroom facilities.

If you still have energy and want to continue farther north, you will eventually come to the monumental rockfall known as the "Giant Stairs"—actually part of the trail and marked as such with white blazes. This section is somewhat difficult and recom-

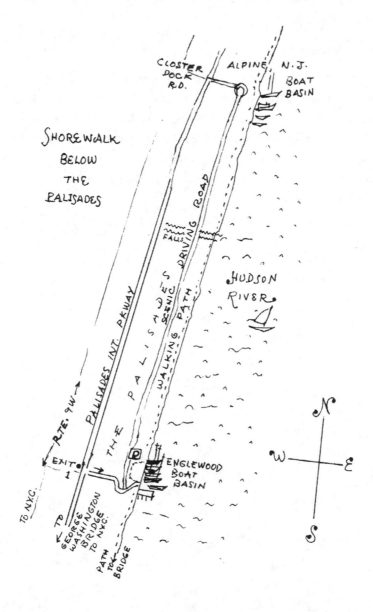

SHOREWALK
BELOW
THE
PALISADES

CLOSTER
DOCK
RD.

ALPINE N.J.

BOAT
BASIN

FALLS

HUDSON
RIVER

PALISADES INT. PKWAY

RTE. 9W

THE PALISADES SCENIC DRIVING ROAD

WALKING PATH

EXIT
1

ENGLEWOOD
BOAT
BASIN

TO N.Y.C.

TO
GEORGE
WASHINGTON
BRIDGE
TO N.Y.C.

PATH
TO
BRIDGE

N

W   E

S

mended only to those who are agile of foot. After some fifteen minutes of this strenuous rock climbing, you will regain the regular shore path.

After the Walk

You might enjoy driving north to several Hudson River villages after your walk. We suggest Piermont (Outing 28), about 5 miles north of Alpine off of Route 9W (turn right at Tallman Park or 0.5 mile farther at the Piermont sign on your right); or continue on River Road through charming Grand View-on-Hudson on to Nyack, about 3 miles farther north.

03 | Three Mushroom Forays

Cheesequake State Park, Jenny Jump State Forest, and Stokes State Forest

How to Get There: For Cheesequake State Park, take either Interstate 80 from the George Washington Bridge or the New Jersey Turnpike to the Garden State Parkway south. Take exit 120, which is Laurence Harbor Road. Make three right turns: Laurence Harbor Road, Cliffwood Avenue, and Gordon Road. Gordon Road goes right to the entrance. For Jenny Jump State Forest, take I–80 from the George Washington Bridge. Turn off at Route 521 south (exit 12). Drive into Hope and make a left at the light, right on Route 611, and left at Fairview Road to the park. For Stokes State Forest, take I–80 from the George Washington Bridge. Turn at Netcong (exit 27) onto Route 206 north. This road will take you directly to the parklands.

While mushroom walks have long been popular in Europe, they are a recent U.S. discovery. The New Jersey Mycological Society has some 300 members, and their outings are well attended. Among their favorite spots for hunting mushrooms are Cheesequake State Park, Stokes State Forest, and Jenny Jump State Forest. The society has frequent outings to these three locations, among many others, and we encourage you to go on a congenial walk with an expert in attendance (see below for information). While there are more than 30,000 varieties of mushrooms, only a few hundred are known edibles, some of which are gourmet delights. About two dozen are deadly poisonous, and the society's newsletter often describes terrible errors made by those who do not know one mushroom from another. For this reason, and because the society has all the specifics on what to look for and where, we recommend that you join up with them (either as a guest or member) for a mushrooming foray.

The outings of the Mycological Society are listed in advance. You can find out about them at www.njmyco.org. The society is a nonprofit organization that goes on regular forays under experienced leaders on Sunday mornings (starting at 10:00 A.M.) from May to October. Among the delights of a walk with the group are the beautiful locations of these three natural settings, as well as the elaborate mushroom-filled meals the society dishes up at various times. Joint trips with other mycological societies are also arranged in surrounding areas and farther afield, including Massachusetts, the Adirondacks, Long Island, and even abroad. Some of these distant outings last for several days.

The mushroom forays are held rain or shine, so be sure to dress accordingly. You should take paper bags (never plastic, which could damage the mushrooms) or waxed paper, a knife, and a basket. Hiking shoes and mosquito repellent are recommended. You should also take a picnic lunch. The leader will explain to you the proper system for cutting, identifying, sorting, and preserving your mushrooms. Collectors are encouraged to bring cameras and/or sketching materials to record their finds. The society will help you with identification charts and other material. Do not bring alcohol or dogs.

We recommend this sort of excursion primarily to adults. Both Stokes and Jenny Jump state parks are quite hilly, so you should be comparatively energetic and surefooted, but the mushroomers take their time as they hunt. This is not a walk to hurry through! The best season for mushrooming is late summer and fall. The right time and location for the prized morel, for example, is researched by the organization and trips are planned accordingly.

🍄 THREE MUSHROOM HUNTING AREAS 🍄

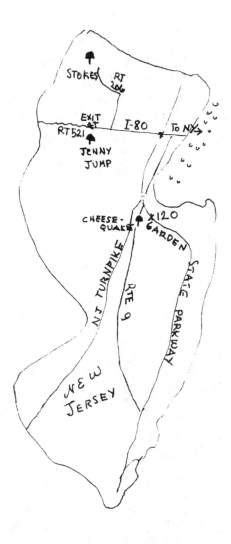

We want to reiterate the advice of the experts: Don't pick and eat any mushroom unless you have the advice of a knowledgeable guide! These are among the few walks that we don't encourage you to do on your own.

After the Walk

If you enjoy picking your own produce—including strawberries, squash, zucchini, and pumpkins—you'll like Four Sisters Winery, not far from Jenny Jump State Forest, on Route 519 near Belvidere. (For information call 908–475–3671.) This is a large produce farm that welcomes you from May to the end of November. Fall brings pumpkins, apples, and hayrides.

04 | An Indoor Garden

Doris Duke Gardens, Somerville

How to Get There: Take the George Washington Bridge to Interstate 80, to Interstate 287 south, to exit 17 at the junction with Route 206 south, to the Somerset Shopping Center. The gardens are located 1.25 miles south of the shopping center, with the entrance on the right. From midtown Manhattan, you can take the New Jersey Turnpike south to I–287 north.

During the cold winter months, no outing is more cheerful than visiting these splendid interconnected hothouses about an hour from New York. The Duke Gardens are part of the estate of Doris Duke, the tobacco heiress, and are one of New Jersey's major attractions. From the moment you drive through the imposing iron gates with their black eagles on top, you feel as if you had entered a magical world of free-roaming deer, exotic flowers, and mythical trees. The fact that you are picked up at the entrance in a van and transported to this fantasy environment adds to the special ambiance.

The conservatories are surrounded by acres of woodsy parkland, with trees planted in formal rows, reminiscent of a European estate. The greenhouses themselves, built in the late nineteenth century for family use, are beautiful. Their ornate glass structure is in an Edwardian conservatory style that is carried into several of the indoor gardens.

The full acre of display gardens was opened to the public in 1964. The Duke family maintains strict control over the management of the estate, and there are many regulations to protect the environment and the valuable plants.

Each of the eleven hothouses has a different theme. You walk from one to the next (in the company of a knowledgeable guide and several other visitors) in about one hour's time. These are total landscape environments that follow the traditions of various countries and eras; there are statuary, rock paths, bridges, and pagodas, as well as a profusion of exotic flowers, shrubs, and trees.

This is a walk that we highly recommend for all adults, including the elderly. Although it is not difficult, women are advised to wear flat shoes, as the footing is sometimes awkward over occasional rocky paths. We do not suggest that you bring children, unless they are particularly interested in plants. It is definitely a decorous walk in which everything is rare and special. Cameras are not allowed, nor should you touch anything. There are neither eating or drinking facilities, nor are there picnic grounds.

The gardens are open daily from October through the end of March from noon to 4:00 P.M. To visit the gardens you must make advance reservations by calling (908) 722–3700. Call about a week ahead of time. There is an entrance fee. You are not allowed to wander at will, but must accompany a tour (limited to ten people). You can also visit the palatial Duke Mansion and experience its reknown Southern charm.

The Walk

Park next to the entrance gate and wait to be picked up by a van, which takes you to the visitor center. From there your escort takes you to the entrance of the conservatories.

The first stop, the Italian garden, is a wonderful beginning. It includes luxuriant blooms of mimosa, bird-of-paradise, orange and pink bougainvillea, Italian statuary and fountains, gravel paths, and an aura of nineteenth-century romance.

From there you go to the American colonial garden, more orderly and classical, with well-groomed hedges, baby's tears

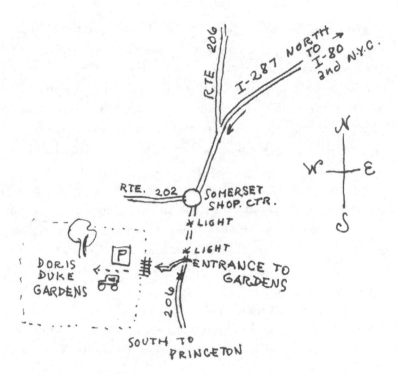

ground cover, camellia bushes, huge rounded magnolias, and hanging pink and white petunias. White latticework and brick-trimmed paths add to the colonial flavor.

The next conservatory—the Edwardian garden—is filled with orchids of every size and brilliant color. White, purple, and magenta blossoms are set off by the deep green of rubber plants and palms in the warm, humid surroundings. The orchids are supplied by other greenhouses on the grounds. This is the quintessential garden of turn-of-the-century romantic novels.

The formal French garden is next. Eighteenth-century lattice-work surrounds this charming, orderly arrangement of stone paths, niches, ivy-festooned columns, statuary, delicate fountains, and wonderful flowery designs including a giant fleur-de-lis of brightly colored plants arranged in the style of the gardens of Versailles.

A group of English gardens follows. There is an herb garden, a rockery, a topiary garden, and a marvelous freestyle annual garden with wonderful color combinations.

Next, contrasting with this brilliance, is the desert garden with a dirt floor and giant cactuses reaching up to the glass ceiling. The ambiance is that of the American Southwest: brown and gray-green tones in knobby, fantastic shapes, giving the visitor the sense of wild, untamed nature.

We then come to the Chinese garden, an oasis of peace and tranquillity. Not as colorful as the European-style flower gardens, it is nonetheless one of the most appealing. Rock formations and goldfish in small ponds, delicate arching stone bridges, mysterious grottoes for contemplation, leaning willows, and a zigzag walk to ward off evil spirits are among the engaging aspects of this traditional Chinese garden.

The Japanese garden is more stylized, with an elegant teahouse, tiny running streams, a miniature wooden bridge, a contemplation area with carefully raked soil to represent waves, and the classic gnarled tree forms of Japanese landscape.

An impressive Indo-Persian garden comes next. The most striking feature is its geometric design, from the patterned cutout white walls and long reflecting pool to the crisp designs made by the yellow, orange, and white flowers and citrus trees. Though it represents an Islamic summer palace garden, it seems almost like an illustration to a fairy tale.

The tropical rain forest garden is a mass of jungle plants of many different sizes and shapes of green, with an occasional ladyslipper orchid hidden in the foliage. Spanish moss, banana plants, and huge elephant ears proliferate.

The semitropical garden in the Mediterranean style is the last. Many kinds of purple flowers decorate the edges of the brick paths and terrace, while gloxinias and gardenias in large urns and hanging bougainvillea add brilliant color to the gray-green ferns. Your own garden might seem rather pale after this visit!

After the Walk

After your walk you might want to drive the 17 miles south to visit Princeton University. See Outing 10.

05 | A Neoclassical Delight
Georgian Court College, Lakewood

How to Get There: Take either Interstate 80 from the George Washington Bridge or the New Jersey Turnpike to the Garden State Parkway south to exit 91. Bear right after the toll plaza and proceed through the first intersection (Burnt Tavern Road) to the next traffic light, at County Line Road, which you take for approximately 5 miles to Route 9. Turn left (south) on Route 9 and continue to Ninth Street. Turn right on Ninth Street and proceed through the Forest Avenue intersection to Lakewood Avenue. The entrance to the college at 900 Lakewood Avenue is on your right.

The name "Georgian Court" suggested to us an eighteenth-century setting in an English countryside, with a stately home, arched bridges over gently flowing water, white marble statues, and formal gardens. We were both astonished and delighted to find exactly such a place hidden away in Ocean County, New Jersey, a treasure for explorers and art lovers, as well as more than 1,000 college students.

Georgian Court College is a beautifully situated campus that was once a very large private estate. It is enclosed by walls along a wide shady street, and when you enter its palatial gates, you come directly upon a setting of such felicitous proportions and so many neoclassical sculptures that you find it hard to equate with the general run-of-the-mill American college campus. Instead of modern kinetic sculpture, you find a fountain statue of Apollo; instead of hard trodden paths from dorm to dorm, you find stone walkways through formal sunken flower beds and a Japanese teahouse.

22

The college (an undergraduate Catholic women's institution, with coed night and graduate divisions) was once the home of George Jay Gould, the financier and railroad magnate. Its 175 acres were purchased in 1896. Gould hired a noted architect, Bruce Price, to design the home in the outskirts of the "winter resort" of Lakewood.

The mansion itself (now a college building) was constructed of gray stucco with white terra-cotta brick, marble, and wood. The interior of the original building is elegantly panelled and maintained. There is an indoor marble pool, and outdoors, where the grounds were designed to match the Georgian-era architecture, there is a lagoon and sunken garden and a majestic promenade.

Gould's son, Kingdon Gould, sold the magnificent estate to the Sisters of Mercy in 1924, and though they transformed it into an educational institution, happily they left its distinctive character intact. In 1985 Georgian Court College was declared a National Historic Landmark.

The Walk

The estate is situated along the banks of Lake Carasaljo in the pines area of south-central New Jersey. As you enter the gates, you will come first to the Italian, or classical, garden, which harmonizes so nicely with the architecture of the original mansion. This elliptical formal garden consists of some sixteen meticulously maintained flower beds bordered by boxwood. A Japanese garden, created in 1925, includes a teahouse, wooden bridges, and shrubbery.

As you leave the flower gardens and walk on into the center of the campus, you will find the rolling green lawns dotted with pathways and classical marble sculptures. The most notable is the Apollo Fountain (1902) designed by John Massey Rhind, a sculptor of public monuments and statues. Its white marble

horses emerge dramatically from the water into the mist created by eight fountains. The bronze figure of Apollo heroically
commands their ascent.

A flight of wide marble steps takes you down to the lake edge
and connects the original sunken garden and lagoon. A promenade in the opposite direction (leading to classroom and library
buildings) is flanked on either side by classical sculptures.

Georgian Court College is open to visitors who wish to walk
around the campus. For information call (732) 362–2200.

After the Walk

Upon leaving Lakewood you will be near two delightful shore
communities: Ocean Grove (see Outing 07) and Spring Lake,
just fifteen minutes south of Ocean Grove. Also in the vicinity
is Allaire Village (see Outing 01), a picturesque deserted town.
On your way home you might enjoy a stop at Deep Cut Park
Horticultural Center, located at 352 Red Hill Road, Middletown
(732–671–6050). This is a garden with an unusual past and
pleasing ambiance.

06 | A Short Brookside Stroll in the Woods
Jones Road Park, Englewood

How to Get There: From the George Washington Bridge, take Route 4 west to the first exit (Jones Road). Go north (right turn) on Jones Road for several blocks. The park is on your right.

Once the wooded property of a private estate, this unusually nice hillside has a brook, its own waterfall, and a pond at the top. The path, beginning with a picnic and playing area, soon becomes surprisingly away-from-it-all, considering that you are only three or four blocks from the roar of the highway you came on. The trail, nicely marked with white blazes, is slightly hilly at all times, but the going is easy and the brook with its big boulders is always right beside you. For a pleasantly uncrowded woodland site literally only five minutes from the George Washington Bridge, you can't do better, unless you want a more extended walk. This is not a long hike, perhaps half an hour at most.

There is a large, flat, grassy play area below the woodland climb, where you can cook out or play Frisbee or watch the ducks on the stream. An ideal place to take children, this park is popular with young people from the neighborhood, but they do not seem to leave the flat area for the hilly climb. However, kids love the path up along the shallow running brook, which is fun to climb over (or fall into, as one of ours did once). At the top you'll see the mansion to which this parkland formerly belonged, as well as the pond that supplies the ever-running waterfall and stream.

You might want to bring a picnic or the makings of a cookout and make a day of it, as there are tables and grills. (There are

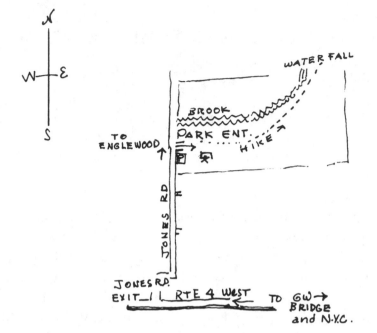

also many refreshment spots in nearby Englewood.) You can enjoy this walk at any time of year; of course, it is deserted in late fall and winter.

The Walk

Leave your car right on Jones Road, parked as near as possible to the fence. Walk directly across the park, following the brook toward the woods. The trail has a white blaze at the entrance just to the right of the stream. The footing is mostly pine needles and mulch, and is pleasant going. There are one or two step-ups, but nothing difficult. At the top you'll find a great flat boulder for sitting and contemplating the waterfall and pond. You can continue at the top for a short distance around the pond, but soon you realize that houses are not far away. An ideal outing for families with young children who would find a longer walk tiring, this one offers a nice combination of playground, brook, forest, and pond.

After the Walk

You might want to combine this visit with another nearby park outing: Fort Lee Historic Park. This park, set right atop the Palisades just south of the George Washington Bridge, is the site of a Revolutionary War fort, and it contains a reconstructed series of structures, military defenses, and even a little cabin where sometimes you'll find a few people dressed as Revolutionary characters roasting a leg of lamb on a spit. Recently a very realistic reenactment of a battle was held at this park. But even if you come on an average day, it's a nice place to view the Hudson, and the historic scenes and setups are interesting and quite well done. To get there from Jones Road Park, go back to Route 4 toward the George Washington Bridge, taking the last Fort Lee exit, which will bring you to Main Street. The park is at the very easternmost end of Main Street, at Hudson Terrace, as, of course, it fronts on the river cliffs. There is a small charge in season for parking.

07 | A Methodist Village on the Shore
Ocean Grove

How to Get There: From midtown Manhattan, take the New Jersey Turnpike south to exit 11 onto the Garden State Parkway south. Take exit IOOB and Route 33 east. Follow the signs to Ocean Grove. From the George Washington Bridge, take Interstate 80 to the Garden State Parkway and follow the same directions as above.

The village of Ocean Grove is a one-of-a-kind shore community. When you think of taking a walk in most shore towns near New York City, you usually find busy, commercial places with little charm. Not so with Ocean Grove. Located on the New Jersey shore one hour's drive south of the city, it contrasts sharply with its neighbors. This is a picturesque town of delightful Victorian gingerbread houses, small hotels, and tiny shops lining pleasantly shaded streets. A fine, wide promenade runs along the oceanfront. Of note is a giant architectural wonder—the Great Auditorium—and dozens of little painted structures for camp meetings.

Ocean Grove's location is what appealed to its founders, a group of Methodist ministers and laypeople who, in 1869, came from Philadelphia to conduct a revival meeting. They pitched their tents in this quiet ocean retreat, creating a religious seaside resort in which to pursue annual summer meetings in relative isolation. Facing the ocean and flanked on both sides by two small lakes (Wesley Lake and Fletcher Lake), they thought the area was "removed from the dissipations and follies of fashionable water places." By 1874 the tent community—known as the "little canvas village"—included about 200 ministers during the height of the season and almost 700 tents with permanent floors and small kitchens.

The Methodist Camp Meeting Association, which ran the community, remained a private association so that it could maintain strict control over the inhabitants of the resort. Lots were leased for ninety-nine years, with the option to renew. Strict regulations included no alcohol, smoking, organ grinders, peddlers, vendors, or carriages on the beach; no swearing in boats on Lake Wesley; no newspapers on Sunday; no dancing; and no card playing. The gates of the resort closed daily at 10:00 P.M. and remained closed all day on Sunday. In fact, no one could do much of anything on Sunday—except attend religious meetings. Trains were not allowed to stop at the Ocean Grove–Asbury Park station (much to the annoyance of the inhabitants of Asbury Park), and no one could enter the community on Sunday except on foot (over the footbridges of Wesley Lake). Indeed, President Ulysses S. Grant, who once visited his mother and sister on a Sunday at their rented Ocean Grove cottage, was obliged to walk into town, like anyone else. His carriage waited for him outside the town gates.

There were a few recreational outlets for visitors to Ocean Grove, however. They were allowed to stroll on the boardwalk and go boating on Wesley Lake. For some time the town fathers thought of banning swimming altogether (because of the inevitable disrobing it entailed), but they agreed to it, reluctantly, with some conditions. (Of course, swimming was forbidden on Sundays.)

Life in Ocean Grove centered around the auditorium (which you can still visit), an immense and curious edifice built in 1894 to accommodate 10,000 people and a 500-member choir. (It was constructed without nails in imitation of Solomon's temple in the Bible.) Here, during camp meetings, religious services were held daily on a continuous basis. Ocean Grove still holds

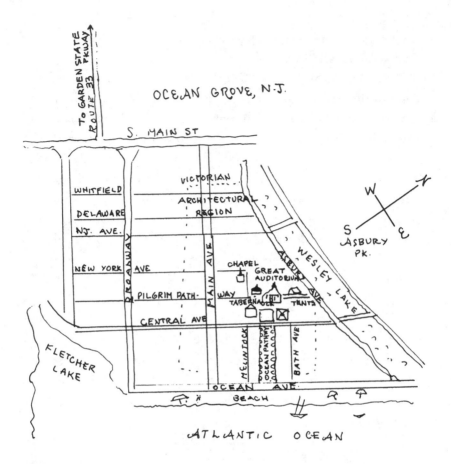

religious and musical programs in this auditorium; indeed, the town remains a religious retreat for many, who still set up tents in summer. Although its blue laws have disappeared, it maintains a pristine and pure quality, which adds to its charm. (It was this special ambiance that appealed to Woody Allen, when he chose it as the location for his film *Stardust Memories* some years ago.)

We think that wandering around this unspoiled town, with its wonderful boardwalk and refreshing ocean breezes, makes for a pleasant outing for just about anyone, young or old. The atmosphere is relaxed and casual, conducive to a leisurely stroll.

Unless people-watching is your favorite sport, we recommend a visit to Ocean Grove off-season, for even here there is inevitably more congestion and activity during the summer months. (And driving to and from the Jersey Shore in summer can be a nightmare.) For information on the village and walking tours, call (732) 774–1869.

The Walk

Park your car wherever you can, preferably along Main Avenue in the center of town. We recommend that you pick up a walking map, available at most real estate agencies and shops along the street. On Main Avenue you'll find many small stores and an array of Victorian houses with gingerbread porches, painted in the most original color combinations. Walk toward the ocean for your stroll on the uncluttered boardwalk, where you'll see a fishing pier and two wide and well-maintained bathing beaches.

After you have filled your lungs with the clean ocean air, you can begin your exploration of the rest of the town. Don't miss Ocean Pathway, a picture-postcard street lined with trees and park benches. You can understand why this street is often photographed—rarely do you have the opportunity to see such a collection of charming and unusual Victorian houses. Make a detour or two to discover some of the other quaint streets that run parallel to Ocean Pathway, starting at Ocean Avenue. Of course, the part of town that is of particular interest is the religious complex, including the Great Auditorium, the Tabernacle, Founders Park, Thornley Chapel, and the remains of some of the tents. You can reach these surprisingly offbeat buildings by walking on Pilgrim Pathway, Central Avenue, or their cross streets. There are squares, pleasant parks, and curious little streets to see at every turn, and you can meander about as long as you like.

Finally, you might enjoy walking across Wesley Lake (toward Asbury Park) on the same bridges that were used by many a

Sunday walker a hundred years ago. You'll notice a sharp contrast between the well-preserved Ocean Grove and its nearby urban neighbor.

After the Walk

After your walk you might enjoy a visit to Allaire Village (see Outing 01) or to Spring Lake, another pleasant waterfront village, about fifteen minutes south of Ocean Grove.

08 | Total Fitness Trail
Shark River County Park, Monmouth County

N
W———E
S

How to Get There: From midtown Manhattan, take the New Jersey Turnpike south to exit 11 onto the Garden State Parkway south. From the George Washington Bridge, take Interstate 80 to the Garden State Parkway. Take exit 100B onto Route 33 east for a few minutes. Turn right at Schoolhouse Road and follow the signs for Shark River County Park, which will be on your right.

You may think you are a fit walker, but you haven't tried anything until you've completed the Fitness Trail at Shark River County Park. Unlike steep climbs that test only your hiking endurance, this trail is a real workout for the total physical fitness buff. We hasten to add that this is also a very pretty walk, even if you just amble through and ignore the fearsome instructions you'll find at every turn.

The trail combines jogging, exercising, and a balanced program of total fitness along a trail of about 1.5 miles. There are thirty-two exercise stations, each with instructions, a course marker, and an apparatus where necessary. You can monitor your heartbeat at regular intervals, following the instructions provided. There are both competitive and less competitive levels. The trail stresses flexibility (for greater coordination in sports), muscle tone (to strengthen and build up your muscles), and cardiovascular conditioning.

Meanwhile, you are walking (or running) on a fairly flat, sandy trail, with scrub pines and dune vegetation typical of the Atlantic shoreline. This pleasant walk is nice in any season and is usually quite deserted, for obvious reasons. (We did see one poor soul emerging from the trail with a sprained ankle.) Following is

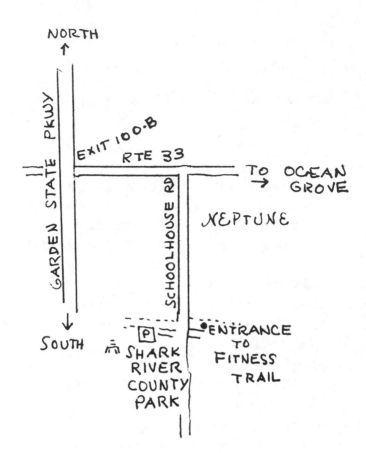

more about the struggles that await anyone brave enough to attempt a full-scale assault on the trail.

Obviously, if you intend to follow the instructions, you should be in excellent physical shape. Of course, you can pick and choose which exercises you wish to do and can walk instead of run from one station to the next. Children with good energy will love the challenges of this outing and will never be bored. Be sure to wear your running shoes (if you're going to run) and comfortable exercise clothes, and take along a stopwatch if you are a competitive athletic type. There are regular nature trails across the road (in the same park), and picnic grounds, so you can bring your own refreshments. The park is open from 8:00 A.M. until dusk, year-round.

The Walk

Park your car in the lot and cross the road away from the picnic area. There are signs indicating where the fitness trail begins and explaining its use. At first you will see only an ordinary woodsy path, but soon exercise no. I appears. After you have completed your first stretches numerous times (they tell you how many of everything to do), you are horrified to realize there are thirty-one more such activities planned for you! Among them are leg bends, pushups, step-ups, a vault, balance beam, stretches, jumps, back exercises, monkey bars, and breathing exercises. You are expected to run or jog from station to station. Periodically you test your heartbeat, understanding that you should stop exercising if you do not meet the recommendations. The apparatuses used for the exercises are discreetly unobtrusive; made of weathered wood, they sit in woodsy alcoves to the side of the trail. The path makes a circle, bringing you back to the same place from which you started when you were young and fresh—and less fit!

After the Walk

After your workout, visit the two Jersey shore villages of Ocean Grove (see Outing 7) and Spring Lake. These are two of the nicest and least spoiled communities on this northern part of the coast, and both have wonderful ocean beaches for walking or swimming, though some areas of the beach are restricted to residents.

09 | A Stroll through a Moravian Village
Hope

How to Get There: From the George Washington Bridge, take Interstate 80 west, exit at Route 521 south (exit 12), and go for a couple of miles until you come to Hope.

It comes as a surprise to many who are only familiar with urban and suburban New Jersey that a good part of the state is rural, with rolling hills and farmlands. As you drive through these areas, you occasionally come across some quaint little towns and villages that have their own particular charm. Hope is among these picturesque villages.

The town, with its Moravian heritage, has an especially intriguing history. The Moravians—a pious, hardworking religious sect from Moravia and Bohemia (now Czechoslovakia)—came to the United States beginning in 1735 to escape persecution. In 1768 one Samuel Green offered a group of Moravians 1,000 acres of land on which to build a settlement. They paid 1,000 pounds sterling.

The community developed fully by about 1774, when a plan was drawn up by the bishop of the mother church in Europe; Hope was one of the first planned communities in this country. (The town plan remains virtually intact today.) The large stone gristmill at the bottom of High Street was one of the town's earliest structures. The limestone Gemeinhaus (corner of Union and High Streets), built a few years later, was at first a community center and place of worship, later a courthouse, and finally a bank.

During the Revolutionary War the Moravians, like the Quakers, were conscientious objectors and refused to fight.

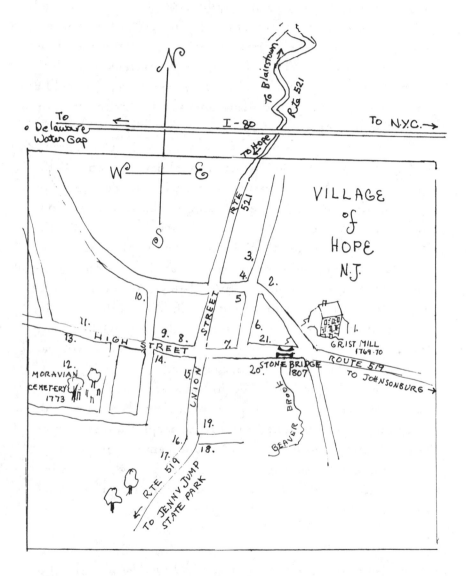

However, they provided excellent nursing care for the wounded

Unfortunately, the settlement of Hope did not last long. By 1791 a serious decline began, and by 1799 the population had been reduced from 147 to only 84. In 1807, after a severe smallpox epidemic, the Moravians decided to sell their community for $48,000. The remaining Moravians moved to Bethlehem, Pennsylvania. Before their departure, they held a final worship service in the Gemeinhaus and at the cemetery on Easter Sunday, April 17, 1808.

This village of stone buildings has remained much the same to this day, and you will enjoy its unusual flavor as you walk the narrow streets. As of our last visit, there was no place to eat or drink in or near the village. We suggest that you bring your own picnic or eat before or afterward at the Martha Washington Pub in nearby Blairstown. You might want to pick up a simple guide to the town, available at several shops, or use the numbered tour guide outlined below. Although an easy walk, Hope is not recommended for children unless they are interested in history and architecture. It's a quiet town with few distractions, and there's a quaint cemetery where you can make grave rubbings of the early markers.

Autumn is lovely here. The hillsides and surroundings of Hope are spectacular if you catch them at the right time. You will find maples (including the striped maple), pines, various kinds of birch, elms, beech, aspens, and hemlocks in the vicinity, and in the fall—and spring—the landscape is glorious. Birds love this tree-filled region. For information and guided tours, call (908) 459–9177 or (908) 459–4884.

The Walk

As you walk around Hope, note some of the features typical of Moravian architecture: the economical use of cut stone (used only in cornerstones or quoins and around doors and windows), redbrick window arches and chimneys, some limestone window arches, and, in some cases, two-story attics that make for balanced design proportions.

A walking tour of Hope should start at the gristmill, at the foot of High Street. (Numbers are keyed to map.)

1. Gristmill (1769–70). Oldest building in the village. During the Revolutionary War it was used to grind grain for Washington's troops.
2. Moravian distillery (1775). Rye whiskey and beer were produced on the ground floor; the brewmaster and his family occupied the second floor. Unfortunately, only a part of the building is still in existence.
3. Farmhouse and barn (1775–76). Oldest remaining residence.
4. Peter Worbass, the first settler in Hope, built a log cabin in 1769 on this site. The cellar of the existing house might have been part of his cabin.
5. Site of the Moravian log tavern (1773). George Washington visited in 1782. A church was later (1841) built on this site; the present building was destroyed by fire in 1918 and rebuilt in the 1950s as a community center.
6. Moravian longhouse (1771). One of the earliest stores occupied this site.
7. Moravian store and residence (1776). Built by Frederick Leinbach, Peter Worbass's successor as town manager, when it seemed that Hope would be a thriving community.
8. House (1787).
9. House (1785).
10. House (1775). The second house built by the community. Later, in 1807, it was used as the schoolhouse.
11. House (1774–76).
12. Moravian cemetery. Contains sixty-two graves, all very simple and plain. On each slab you can read the name, birth and death dates, and a number that corresponds to the list of burials in the Moravian Archives at Bethlehem, Pennsylvania.

13. Site of St. John's United Methodist Church (1832). The present building dates from 1879.
14. St. Luke's Episcopal Church (1832), built of native limestone. Note the interior spiral staircase, supposedly copied from a design by Sir Christopher Wren.
15. Gemeinhaus (1781). The place of worship for the community. There were separate staircases for men and women that led to the actual church room on the second floor. The first floor included the living quarters of the pastor and a small school for boys.
16–18. Moravian houses (all dating from 1776).
19. The Moravian school building, also known as the Single Sisters Choir, was the last structure built by the Moravians in Hope (1803). It housed the colony's unmarried women and was also, for a short time, used as a school for boys.
20. Stone Bridge (1807). Not built by the Moravians, although it has been called the Moravian Bridge.
21. Hope Historical Society Museum. Once the bridge tollhouse, the museum is open on weekends during the summer.

After the Walk

If you're an adventurous sort, try gliding and hot-air ballooning at Tock's Island Soaring, Inc., on Route 94 just west of Blairstown, which offers rides, rentals, and lessons. In the fall there is apple picking at Race Farm near Blairstown.

Beachers, rowers, and picnickers should enjoy Mount Lake Beach in season. It's a small, pretty lakeside area nestled into the surrounding hills. You can rent rowboats, enjoy the pleasant beach (nice for children), and have a picnic here. Take Union Street north from Hope, make a left on Lake Justit Road to its end, and turn right to Mount Lake Beach.

10 | A University Ramble
Princeton

How to Get There: From midtown Manhattan, take the New Jersey Turnpike to exit 9. Take Route 1 south, then Route 571 west to Princeton. Follow the signs for the university. For information on public transportation, call New Jersey Transit at (800) 772–2222.

Princeton University is not just the prettiest school in our area; it's often called one of the most beautiful in the country. The spacious elegance of the campus—with its great Gothic buildings and archways, geometric pathways, fine modern buildings, grand trees, charming gardens, outdoor sculpture, and lake—and its sense of the gracious past are all easily available to a visiting stroller. The campus provides the visitor with acres to wander through, and the town of Princeton itself includes many wonderful areas. You will have to choose your route by how much time you have, for you could spend several days exploring the many areas here.

The university was founded in 1754; Nassau Hall, at its center, was completed two years later and is still in use. Despite bombardment during the Revolution and two fires, the Continental Congress was able to meet there in 1783, when Princeton served as the nation's capital for four months. The school soon began to add buildings and today is a legendary educational institution, with a fine Gothic chapel (which you should not miss on your walk); the modern Woodrow Wilson School building, designed by Minoru Yamasaki; Maclean House, the home of the university's presidents from 1756 to 1879 and now alumni headquarters; Alexander Hall, a Victorian auditorium;

the twin Whig and Clio debating society Greek Revival buildings; the fine art museum; and dozens of other interesting sites. You can walk across the spacious lawns from one to another, along with students as they stroll to a class or an activity, or read in the shadow of the famous Gothic towers or beside a contemporary sculpture. This traditional university is quintessentially "collegiate," and we guarantee you'll enjoy it.

Princeton, the town, faces the campus across the main street, Nassau Street. Shops and restaurants and a bustling atmosphere contrast with the quiet of the campus; you will enjoy visiting Palmer Square in the center of town, as well as several nonuniversity sites. In addition, two other places outside the campus are worth seeing: the Grover Cleveland Tower and Graduate College with its fine view, and the Institute for Advanced Study, where Albert Einstein and other great thinkers have worked.

The walk suggested below is only one of many possibilities. The university provides guided tours, if you prefer. If not, we advise you to pick up a full campus map (available at Maclean House) and try to follow the route given below. Alternatively, you can leave your car and just wander about the university, noting whichever buildings you happen to pass and perhaps ending your jaunt by Lake Carnegie at the university boathouse, where (in season) you'll see sculls filled with rowers setting off in the swift current.

Any time of year is the right time for this walk. In summer, of course, school is not in session, and you'll miss the full student aura, but the buildings and flowers and shaded walks are all there. (Avoid the major graduation and reunion week in early June and arrival time in mid-September, when parking is impossible.) There are innumerable university events throughout the year, from professional music and theater to sporting events and student performances. You might want to coordinate your visit with such an event. The major football games in the fall come complete with band marching across the campus, tiger mascots, and singing groups performing under hallowed arches. Full information and tickets for such events can be obtained by calling (609) 258–1766.

Princeton is an almost completely flat area, and therefore walking is not tiring, but the distances are quite large. The paths are generally gravel. Families will enjoy this outing, including older children in particular, who might like to imagine themselves as students someday. You need not bring anything special. Every kind of eatery can be found across the street, and you can pick up all sorts of information and maps on the history, courses, and events at the admissions office at 110 West College.

The Walk

We suggest you leave your car outside the campus either at a meter on Nassau Street or in a lot just behind it. Our walk assumes that you are starting off in the center of town at Palmer Square, and entering the gate of the university directly opposite the kiosk. (Numbers are keyed to map.)

1. Maclean House will be the first building on your left. Here you can get an escorted tour of the campus, or a sculpture tour, or just a map to make the tour yourself. For guided tour reservations, call (609) 258–3603. (You can also wait for a tour without a reservation.) Maclean House is itself of interest; it once housed Aaron Burr, as well as university presidents from 1756 to 1879.

2. Princeton University's landmark Nassau Hall will be your next stop. Here, beginning in 1756, American history was made. The Continental Congress met here when Princeton served as capital of the country. Washington's capture of the building in 1777 ended the Battle of Princeton, and he returned to the hall again in 1783 to receive the thanks of the Congress for his conduct of the war. For some fifty years Nassau Hall contained all of Princeton's classrooms and

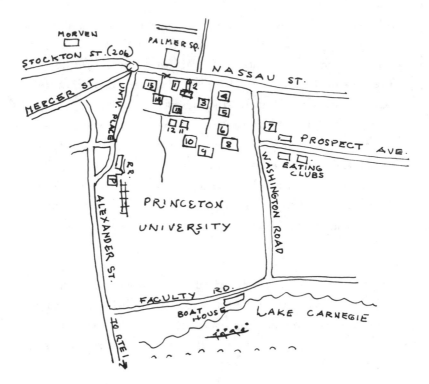

dormitories, as well as its library, dining room, chapel, and kitchen. Behind Nassau Hall is Cannon Green, the quadrangle that is the site of the Big Cannon and now the center of many festivities at the college.

3. East Pyne, the building that houses the student center, is next on your tour. Be sure to go inside and see the rotunda.

4. When you come out of East Pyne, you will see Firestone Library, which houses more than 3.5 million books. One of the world's great university libraries, Firestone is worth entering: It has many special collections and is a fascinating place to visit.

5. A stop at the university chapel is not to be missed. Built between 1925 and 1928, it is the third-largest college chapel in the world. Its Gothic architecture, inspired by the chapel of King's College, Cambridge, England, is enhanced by exquisite

stained-glass windows by American artists. It seats some 2,000 people and is frequently the scene of Princeton weddings.

6. From the chapel, walk through McCosh Hall archway and out onto Prospect Avenue, where the mansions housing the university "eating clubs" for upperclassmen and women are located.

7. At the corner of Prospect and Washington Road, you'll find the Woodrow Wilson School, a striking contemporary building with a reflecting pool. Designed by Minoru Yamasaki, the building opened in 1960 as the home of the School of Economics, Politics, and History. Several notable sculptures are on display here.

8. Turn back toward the School of Architecture, completed in 1963 and housing an architectural laboratory, as well as a gallery and studios.

9. Prospect House and Garden are an especially handsome part of the campus. For many years the home of university presidents, this fine mansion was built in 1849 and has an illustrious history. It now houses dining and social facilities for the university's faculty and staff, and has attractive, well-tended gardens.

10. The University Art Museum, which is easily recognized by the giant Picasso sculpture in front, is a first-class museum. It is open to the public and includes a notable collection of antiquities, Renaissance paintings, and modern works. It is used by art and art history students, as well as by scholars from around the world.

11–12. These twin buildings in the Greek Revival style are across Cannon Green from Nassau Hall. The halls, called Whig and Clio, originally housed the American Whig Society and the Cliosophic Society, the nation's oldest college debating and literary clubs. Extracurricular life revolved around the societies in the nineteenth century, and a number of notable future politicians debated in them. Today they are still the scene of debates and lectures.

13. West College, constructed in traditional design as a dormitory complex, is typical of the campus style. It is now home to university offices, including the admissions office (where you can pick up a variety of brochures and guidebooks).

14. Alexander Hall, with its Richardson Auditorium, is an architectural oddity and campus landmark. It was the first building erected by the Presbyterian Church in the United States for seminary purposes. Its rounded walls and unusual architecture make it well worth visiting, and you will often find an interesting event going on within.

15. Holder Hall is a typical residential building and is part of Rockefeller College. Walk into the quad and you'll get a sense of what living in the university undergraduate area is like. The cloistered walkways and arches are open to wander through, and you're apt to think, *this* is what colleges are supposed to look like!

Cross through the arch back out onto Nassau Street and to your parking meter, but don't go home yet. Other campus sites worth visiting are Princeton Inn College, Palmer Stadium, and the boathouse.

In the neighborhood are a number of "don't miss" sites: the Institute for Advanced Study, the Theological Seminary, the Graduate College, and the homes of Thomas Mann, Woodrow Wilson, Albert Einstein, and Paul Robeson. A map obtainable at Maclean House will direct you to these locations. It also lists a number of old houses in the township and the Princeton Cemetery, where the earliest stones date from 1760.

Finally, you might want to see Morven. This house, now a national landmark, was built by Richard Stockton, a signer of the Declaration of Independence. It is the official residence of the governors of New Jersey and has hosted nine presidents and a variety of kings, queens, and other luminaries.

11 | A Fragrant and Sensory Garden

Colonial Park, Somerset County

How to Get There: From the George Washington Bridge, take Interstate 80 west to Interstate 287 south. After passing Bound Brook, take Route 527 (Easton Avenue). Go right on Cedar Grove Lane, then go right again on Weston Road to Elizabeth Avenue. The entrance to the park is on your left on Elizabeth Avenue. From midtown Manhattan, take the Lincoln Tunnel to the New Jersey Turnpike south to I–287, and follow same directions as above.

This extraordinary pair of gardens—one all roses, the other a fragrance and sensory garden—are really special, especially for those who are blind or physically challenged. While it forms only a small one-acre part of a large and spacious county park in Franklin Township, it has a rare quality all its own. Once part of a private estate, the gardens were developed by a horticulturalist when they became part of the public park.

The more unusual of the two gardens is the fragrance and sensory garden. Newly designed with Braille plaques and a low handrail, this garden includes especially interesting flowers and plants to smell and touch. Each example has an unusual quality, such as the soft, fuzzy lamb's ears, the fragrant lavender plant, and the tasty mint. As you make your way around the garden, you can feel and smell and even taste these odd, fragrant plants and guess what they are, or read the small plaques. There are soft, spongy plants, prickly plants, and aromatic lemony plants. The flat walkway is made to accommodate the physically and visually impaired, with flagstone paving and intersecting strips of brick to indicate changes in direction. There are many

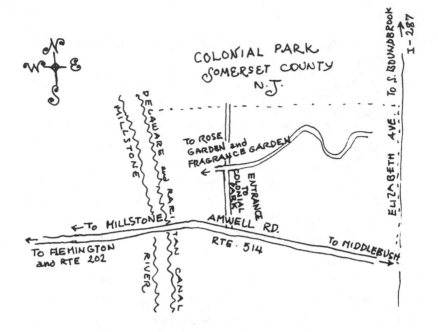

charming arbored benches for resting. We also recommend this walk for families with children, as it is quite short.

Adjoining the Sensory and Fragrance Garden is the Rose Garden, and what a rose garden it is! Described as "an encyclopedia of roses," the collection includes 4,000 rosebushes (275 varieties) that bloom from early June all the way into fall. One of the sections is called Grandmother's Garden and contains old hybrid perpetual and hybrid tea roses, some of which date back to the 1820s. Another part has climbing roses, while the Dutch Garden is in the style of a formal rose garden in Holland. It is a beautifully designed garden that is constantly in bloom during the long season. Everything is identified. A walk through it on the flagstone paths can be broken with little rests on arbored benches. For the rose fancier, this is a blissful stroll.

If you are of a romantic disposition, you'll find that both gardens have a touch of another time and place about them. We did—on a hot summer day, with the various flowery aromas wafting through the air, and the cool shaded benches inviting us to rest for a moment.

Colonial Park is a vast place, rather overdeveloped, with something for everyone seeking recreation, from paddleboats to a small foresty nature walk, a nice lilac garden, picnic tables, tennis courts, and a playground, in addition to the gardens described above. There are other walks in the park, of course, including a stroll through the arboretum. Guided tours are also available.

The hours are daily from 8:00 A.M. to sunset, from June I to November I. For more information call (732) 873–2459.

12 | Landscape Elegance in a Rustic Region
Skylands Botanical Garden, Ringwood

How to Get There: From the George Washington Bridge, take Route 4 west to Route 17 north. Follow the signs for Ringwood just after Shepard Lake on Morris Avenue.

Skylands, New Jersey's state botanical garden, is aptly named. To visit this vast site deep in the Ramapo Mountains, you must drive up and up on a winding road—toward the sky.

Finally you reach what appears to be (and once was) a grand, yet surprisingly informal, country estate, complete with elegant Tudor-style buildings, delightful gardens, long allées, and broad vistas. The beautifully designed landscape combines formal and naturalistic areas—separated by a magnificent crab apple walk—broad panoramic views, and even pieces of sculpture. The ambiance is low-key and friendly. Exploring these spacious grounds (some 125 acres of them) is a most pleasant, even joyful experience, particularly on a bright spring day, when the many blooming plants add their enchantment.

Skylands' origins as a gentleman's working farm are still apparent in its rustic, yet genteel, charms. Francis Lynde Stetson a prominent, turn-of-the-twentieth-century New York lawyer, called his property "Skyland Farms." His grounds (which also included the mansion, sweeping lawns, and even a small golf course) were designed by Samuel Parsons Jr., a protégé of Frederick Law Olmsted.

But it was the estate's next proprietor, Clarence McKenzie Lewis, who was responsible for turning Skylands into a botanical

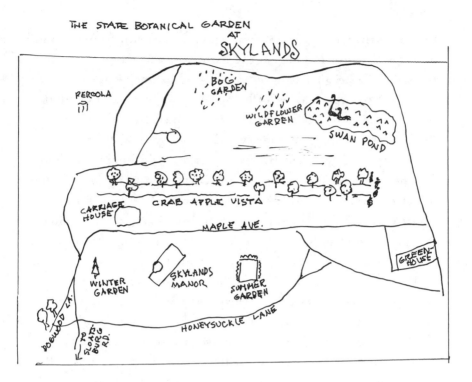

THE STATE BOTANICAL GARDEN
AT
SKYLANDS

PERGOLA

BOG GARDEN

WILDFLOWER GARDEN

SWAN POND

CARRIAGE HOUSE

CRAB APPLE VISTA

MAPLE AVE.

GREEN-HOUSE

WINTER GARDEN

SKYLANDS MANOR

SUMMER GARDEN

DOGWOOD LA.

PIERSON RD. SLOATSBURG

HONEYSUCKLE LANE

showplace. Lewis, an amateur but dedicated botanist, collected plants from all over the world during the 1920s. With his army of gardeners he planted specimens from Afghanistan, Chile, and New Jersey, as well as native New Jersey. Although he engaged landscape architects to design the gardens around the house, he had much to say about which plants should go where. Lewis carefully considered the color, texture, form, and even fragrance of each plant, so that it would be part of a harmonious whole.

In the 1960s New Jersey purchased the property, and in March 1984 the ninety-six acres surrounding the manor house were designated as the state's official botanical garden. For information about hours, tours, and fees, call (973) 962–9534 or visit www.njbg.org.

51

The Walk

Before setting forth on your walk, you might want to pick up a descriptive guide and map at the visitor center, where the helpful staff will be glad to give you any additional information. Among Skylands' many offerings are an Annual Garden, Summer Garden, Azalea Garden, Peony Garden, Lilac Garden, Octagonal Garden, Winter Garden, Magnolia Walk, Crab Apple Vista, Bog Garden, Swan Pond, Wildflower Garden, Heather Garden, a greenhouse collection, and miles of walking to satisfy even the most energetic visitor. The 1920s manor house (made from stone quarried on the estate) can be visited by guided tour only, but you can wander through the broad landscape and individual gardens on your own.

The Winter Garden (which Lewis could enjoy from his library window on even the dreariest wintry day) features a rare collection of some thirty varieties of evergreens. Included are an Atlas cedar, a Jeffrey pine (now grown to giant proportions), an Algerian fir, and an impressive Japanese umbrella pine, a main attraction. You can walk around the trees and admire their different shapes, sizes, and shades of green, gray-blue, gray, and even gold.

The nearby formal Terrace Gardens behind the manor house are like individual outdoor galleries. The Octagonal Garden, so named for its central pool and fountain, includes a charming rock garden; the gracious Magnolia Walk, with its fragrant plantings, leads to the Azalea Garden, resplendent with banks of azaleas and rhododendrons on both sides of a reflecting pool. Beyond lie the Summer, Peony, and Lilac gardens. A good place to take a short rest to plot your next route is on a semicircular stone bench at the end of a grouping of hemlocks in the Peony Garden.

The Crab Apple Vista—an incredible double row of trees that forms the boundary between the gardens near the house and the wilder areas to the east—is undoubtedly Skylands' most enchanting attraction. As you walk on this half-mile stretch, surrounded on each side by over 160 crab apples (whose spring blossoms alone are worth the trip!), you can enjoy wide views of gardens, meadows, woods, and mountains. At the end of the vista, opposite the Horse Chestnut Collection, you'll find the Four Continents statues. Set in a semicircle next to the woods, these time-worn stone forms represent four of the continents. Their style is classical with romantic overtones, and they are based on seventeenth-century works.

From here you can wander through the more informal collections to see rhododendron, heather, and different varieties of wildflowers. Nearby is Swan Pond, where you are more likely to come upon frogs than anything else.

You'll find there is more to discover and do at Skylands than simply a day's worth. Also scheduled are special events and classes in horticulture, nature photography, and nature watercolor painting, all of which will give you the opportunity to experience Skylands from different perspectives.

After the Walk

Just down the road you'll find Ringwood Manor, an unusual estate with an interesting history, a sculpture garden, and a magnificent sweep of green lawns, giant trees, stone walls, formal gardens, orchards, a lake, and forests. Call (973) 962–7031 or visit www.ringwoodmanor.com for details.

Long Island

13 | Through the Meadows to the Beach
Caumsett State Park

How to Get There: From uptown Manhattan, take the Cross Bronx Expressway to the Throgs Neck Bridge to the Cross Island Parkway, to the Long Island Expressway (Interstate 495) east, to Route 110 (exit 49N) north, to Route 25A west to Goose Neck Road, to West Neck Road, to Lloyd Harbor Road, to the park entrance. From midtown Manhattan, take the Midtown Tunnel to the Long Island Expressway and follow the same directions as above.

Caumsett State Park offers an unusually unspoiled and uncrowded trip through meadows of wildflowers and deep woods to a pristine North Shore beach. This is an outing for all seasons. In springtime there are masses of buttercups and other wildflowers amid a romantic Constable-like landscape; in summer, the possibility of a great swim; in fall, the vivid colors of foliage; and in winter, wonderful cross-country skiing.

The great advantage of this walk is its unstructured setup: no lifeguards, no snack bars, no facilities—including no way to shorten the trip back. No motorized vehicles (except by special permit) are allowed. The beach is clean, but somewhat pebbly, and surrounded with real sand dunes. Fishermen are often the only visitors here.

This 1,475-acre park was once the estate of Marshall Field III, the grandson of the founder of the department store. Field, an imaginative philanthropist whose interests included civic and educational pursuits as well as the outdoor life, built this estate in the 1920s as a sort of self-sufficient rural community, with its own water and electrical supply and its own dairy and vegetable farm. Converted to a state park in recent years, Caumsett is an especially serene place for a day away.

Located on a beautiful peninsula stretching into Long Island Sound, the park is essentially flat (elevations rise to only 120 feet above sea level). It includes a freshwater pond, marshes (which account for the rich birdlife), and many dirt and stony paths crisscrossing to the sea. The beach has some great boulders in addition to a fairly pebbly surface. This is not a fine-sand beach.

While all seasons are recommended for this outing, Caumsett is, of course, more crowded in summer. But even on weekends the park is not too busy, and on most weekdays it is positively deserted. On a day that we were there, we met—in the entire day—only one couple fishing and one artist.

This is not a walk with dramatic cliffs and vistas. The mostly level terrain is good for conversation, nature-watching, and other quiet activities. Its length (about 2 miles each way, plus 1 mile along the beach) is not excessive, but the return trip might be hard on small children, due to the lack of public facilities (this, obviously, is one of the things that keeps the beach quite empty). We suggest you pick up a map and brochure at the parking booth.

There are no public concessions, so be sure to take food and beverages (nonalcoholic). Take a bathing suit in summer and plan to change behind some bushes. If you're a birder, take binoculars. Do not bring pets. As for shoes, we recommend good walking shoes or sneakers for the dirt paths, pebbly shoreline, and rocky coastline. While this is not a rigorous walk, the terrain would be hard on bare feet or flimsy shoes. If you like surf fishing, this is the spot, but you need a permit to drive in (though not to fish). If you prefer to bike or jog, you can save energy for exploring the beach. You will find this area pleasant, although the surface is not ideal. Cross-country skiers may also

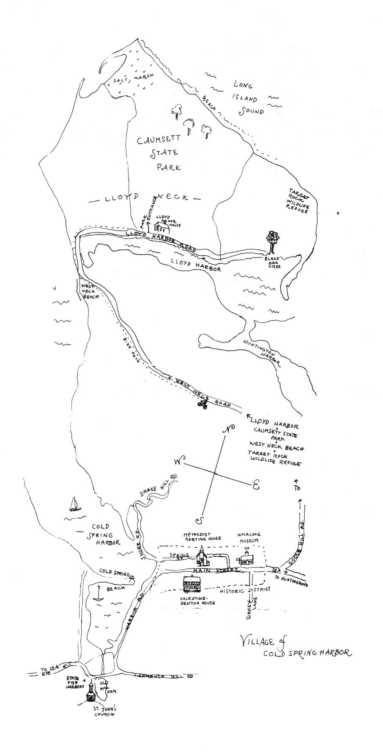

SALT MARSH

LONG ISLAND SOUND

BEACH

CAUMSETT STATE PARK

TARGET ROCK WILDLIFE REFUGE

— LLOYD NECK —

PARK ENTRANCE

LLOYD MANOR HOUSE

LLOYD HARBOR ROAD

LLOYD HARBOR

BLACK OAK TREE

WEST NECK BEACH

BIKE PATH

HUNTINGTON HARBOR

WEST NECK ROAD

← LLOYD HARBOR
CAUMSETT STATE PARK
WEST NECK BEACH
TARGET ROCK WILDLIFE REFUGE

N

W

E

S

↑ TO

SNAKE HILL RD.

COLD SPRING HARBOR

SHORE RD.

GOOSE HILL RD.

METHODIST MEETING HOUSE

WHALING MUSEUM

SPRING

COLD SPRING

MAIN STREET

TO HUNTINGTON →

BEACH

HARBOR RD.

HISTORIC DISTRICT

VALENTINE-DENTON HOUSE

RTE 25A

VILLAGE of COLD SPRING HARBOR

TO 25A RTE.

LAWRENCE HILL RD.

STATE FISH HATCHERY

OLD MILL DAM

ST. JOHN'S CHURCH

take advantage of the trails and bridle paths through the woods, adding variety to their trek.

The park is open daily, sunrise to sunset; there is a small parking fee in season. For information call (631) 423–1770.

The Walk

Park in the lot next to the booth. Set out across the meadow about .03 of a mile, bearing left to pick up a sandy trail (or stay in the meadows, if you prefer). The trail is wide enough to spot easily. As you can see from the official Caumsett Park map, you have many choices of trails to get to the water. If you choose the most direct route, you will go through fields and woods for about 1.5 miles, through dense vine-covered forest and past the marsh on the left. You will have gone almost 2 miles from the start. On the beach, if you bear left, you will come to a point and a cove in about a 0.5 mile. For a longer beach walk, turn right and go about 1 mile to some small steps up to a bluff and a return trail. On the beach enjoy seagulls and wonderful sunbathing rocks where you can stretch out, surrounded by gentle lapping water.

Birders will find an abundance of species in the salt marsh: black-crowned night heron, green heron, egrets, great blue heron, great white heron, osprey, gulls, red-winged blackbird, kingfishers, black ducks, and marsh hawk, as well as sparrows. Nature lovers will enjoy the variety of trees, birds, wildflowers, and shells and colorful stones (great skipping stones) on the beach. Plants in and around the marsh include the endangered prickly pear cactus (which you should not touch!), high-water bush, beach plum, and sea rocket, as well as the more common goldenrod and dandelion.

While there are no formal picnic sites, we recommend (in addition to large beach rocks, where it might be fun to eat with your feet dangling in the water) that you try the charming grassy shaded lookout area atop the bluffs at the far end of the beach, where the path starts home. Walk back via the freshwater pond and Marshall Field House, despite a fairly steep but mercifully short hill. There are several return routes to choose from; consult your map.

After the Walk

This is a great area for sightseeing. In the immediate vicinity, at the end of Lloyd Harbor Road, don't miss the famous 100-foot-tall black oak tree, which is supposed to be the largest of its kind in the country. Also of interest is the Lloyd Manor House, a white colonial building that is open to the public and is also situated nearby on Lloyd Harbor Road.

You might enjoy a visit to the nearby village of Cold Spring Harbor. Its importance as a whaling port in the nineteenth century has left it a legacy of frame buildings on narrow Main Street, surrounded by waterfront country lanes and the marshes typical of this part of Long Island. Its charm lies both in its situation on the water and the bustling center of the village that, despite some trendy boutiques, retains the original scale and architecture of the whaling era.

Try a walking tour of about three blocks on Main Street, with its charming houses of the early and mid-nineteenth century. Don't miss the Methodist Meeting House, built in 1842 to give the village residents their own church; the Conklin house, at 75 Main Street, built in 1720 and the oldest house in town; Manuel Enos's imposing home, at 208 Main Street; and, among many others, the Valentine-Denton house, at 60 Main Street, which was occupied by whaling captains through the years. The Whaling Museum, also on Main Street, is worth a visit. There you will find a completely outfitted whaling boat that will delight children and nostalgics.

Beyond Main Street, on Route 25A near the junction to Route 108, is the Cold Spring Harbor Fish Hatchery and Aquarium, which has interesting exhibits of various kinds.

Outside the immediate vicinity, we recommend the following attractions:

The Heckscher Museum of Art in Huntington, on Prime Avenue and Route 25A, was founded in 1920 and houses a small but excellent collection of American and European paintings. Open year-round, Tuesday through Friday, 10:00 A.M. to 5:00 P.M., and Saturday and Sunday, 1:00 to 5:00 P.M. (summer weekends, 1:00 to 8:00 P.M.). Call (631) 351–3250 for more information.

The Vanderbilt Museum, near Northport, a twenty-four room Spanish Moroccan–style mansion on forty-three wooded acres, is now a natural science museum and planetarium. See Outing 14.

14 | A Fanciful Museum/Estate

Vanderbilt Museum, Centerport

How to Get There: From uptown Manhattan, take the Cross Bronx Expressway to the Throgs Neck Bridge, to the Cross Island Parkway, to the Long Island Expressway (Interstate 495) east, to exit 51N (Deer Park Avenue). Take Deer Park Avenue (Route 231) north for 6 miles to Broadway and across Route 25A, where Broadway becomes Little Neck Road. The estate is on your right, behind white decorative walls, and is clearly marked. From midtown Manhattan, take the Midtown Tunnel to the Long Island Expressway and follow the same directions as above.

When you enter the imposing gates to the Vanderbilt Museum—once the fabled "Eagle's Nest" estate of one of America's most illustrious families—you are transported to an era of glamour, elegance, and privilege in a setting right out of a movie. Located on Long Island's North Shore, where many wealthy families built homes around the turn of the twentieth century, it includes the storybook, fanciful Vanderbilt mansion, a marine museum (housed in the whimsical Hall of Fishes), a planetarium (added much later), six antique marble Corinthian columns in a semicircle near the entrance gate, a charming boathouse, and some forty-three rolling acres overlooking Long Island Sound.

The estate was the home of William Kissam Vanderbilt II (1878–1944), great-grandson of "Commodore" Cornelius Vanderbilt of shipping and railroad fame. What he had begun in 1907 as a relatively modest six-room Japanese cottage was expanded over the years to a much grander twenty-four rooms in elaborate Spanish Moroccan architectural style, with additional wings, courtyards, arcades, a tall domed bell tower, a patio

NORTHPORT BAY

BOATHOUSE

VANDERBILT

PLANETARIUM

MANSION

VISITOR
CENTER

HALL of
FISHES

LITTLE NECK ROAD

TO RTE
25 A

N W E S

THE VANDERBILT MUSEUM

with reflecting pool, formal gardens, and a nearby ten-hole golf course and boathouse. When William Vanderbilt died in 1944, his will stipulated that the estate be donated for "the education and enjoyment of the public," to be used as a museum when his widow no longer wished to live there. A man of surprisingly diverse interests—including architecture, art, anthropology, history, ornithology, ichthyology, sailing, auto racing, and aviation—he was a world traveler, explorer, sportsman, and collector.

The visitor here will be fascinated and delighted by the array of things to view, from mounted animals (hunted by Vanderbilt himself), marine specimens, and dioramas, to fine paintings, rare objects, and unusual furniture—all personally collected by Vanderbilt. Unlike visits to many estates, this one is filled with surprises at every turn and should appeal to most anyone—including, or especially, children. You can walk through the Vanderbilt Marine Museum (Hall of Fishes) on your own and roam about the grounds freely. To visit the mansion itself, you must join a guided tour; the guide provides unusually interesting tidbits of information about the life and times of Vanderbilt.

The planetarium, built in 1971 on the site of what used to be the family tennis courts and now among the largest and best equipped in the country, is open to the public for regular sky shows Fridays, Saturdays, and Sundays, as well as for public viewing after the evening sky shows, weather permitting. Tickets are sold at the planetarium box office half an hour before shows. In addition, the planetarium offers special programs such as live sky talks; school presentations; adult education courses in astronomy, meteorology, and navigation; and programs for the physically and mentally challenged. For information call 631–854–5538.

A visit to the Vanderbilt Museum is recommended for anyone interested in history, art, nature, zoology, or in just poking about and exploring a fascinating side of Americana in a beautiful natural setting with wonderful views of the water. Children will surely be intrigued with the dioramas of natural scenes and the wide assortment of lifelike animals, including enormous crocodiles, whales, insects, and odd fish caught by Vanderbilt in many exotic places.

The mansion tour takes about forty-five minutes and is highly recommended. The rest of your visit depends on how much time you have to spend. The outdoor walk through the spacious grounds is pleasant, even if somewhat hilly. Wear comfortable shoes. There are no concessions or picnic facilities on the grounds, but plenty of cafes and restaurants can be found in Centerport or, even better, in nearby picturesque Northport.

The museum, which is open year-round Tuesday through Sunday from noon to 4:00 P.M., is a popular destination on weekends (especially in summer and fall). We suggest you try to go during the week, if possible (unless you want to see a show at the planetarium). When we visited on a brilliant Friday in mid-

November, we were alone and enjoyed a private guided tour. For further museum information, call (631) 854–5555.

The Walk

After parking your car (near two imposing iron eagles), go to the visitors' reception center to buy your ticket, which includes everything except the planetarium. It is suggested that you first visit the Hall of Fishes. The oldest part of this original and eccentric building dates from 1922, but it was added on to at intervals, making it a sort of Moroccan potpourri. Made of white stucco and colorful tiles, it has four imposing spiral columns next to the front door. The roof of this building was used by the Vanderbilts to tee off onto their private golf course just below. Inside, in one big room, are the colorful tropical marine specimens, as well as giant mounted fish, turtles, a whale, and other animals.

Return to the visitors' reception center for your guided tour of the mansion. (Tours are conducted regularly every fifteen minutes and are designed for average walkers.) You are first shown an interesting model of the entire mansion—including wings, courtyards, and gardens. The model will help you orient yourself in this extensive and labyrinthine structure. (Dollhouse enthusiasts may like this as much as anything on the tour!) Your next stop is the animal museum, a large dark room of dioramas displaying a variety of beasts and birds in lifelike settings, much like the American Museum of Natural History.

Next you enter the mansion itself. The Spanish Moroccan–style house is filled with original furnishings, memorabilia, objects, paintings, and artifacts that were all collected by William Vanderbilt on his travels in Europe and the Orient. The rooms have been kept just as they were when the family lived here. Vanderbilt acquired paintings and furniture based on his own personal tastes rather than on the advice of experts, and he placed them where he felt they looked best. Nothing has been moved or rearranged in any way. It is interesting to see the house in its genuine, lived-in arrangement, rather than as a museum, where things are placed according to periods and styles. The result, for such a grand house, is surprisingly intimate, warm, and friendly. We found the dining room—with its rustic furnishings, hand-carved wooden ceiling, and tile floors—particularly inviting. The bedrooms—including one that was frequently occupied by the Duke and Duchess of Windsor, who were close friends of the second Mrs. Vanderbilt—are cheerful and cozy, with bright fabrics and beautiful Oriental rugs. One of the living rooms features a massive 2,000-pipe organ, which was installed in the 1920s for about $90,000. All of the rooms have views onto courtyards, formal gardens, or Long Island Sound, particularly in winter when the linden trees near the house have lost their leaves. Your last stop indoors is the insect and bird museum, where hundreds of species are displayed and identified. There are also many photographs of the Vanderbilts' exploits.

At the end of the tour, you are invited to explore the grounds further on your own. Walk through the formal gardens, including the charming English boxwood garden with its intricate patterns; see the reflecting pool and surrounding garden; and visit the rose garden, which is most fragrant and appealing in summer. You can wend your way down to the boathouse, a French-style building at the water's edge, where the Vanderbilts entertained afternoon yachting guests.

After the Walk

This is a scenic part of Long Island, not far from several places worth visiting: Teddy Roosevelt's home at Sagamore Hill (see Outing 16), the picturesque town of Northport and nearby Eatons Neck (see Outing 17), or Caumsett State Park (see Outing 13).

15 | An Arboretum Outing
Planting Fields Arboretum, Oyster Bay

How to Get There: From uptown Manhattan, take the Cross Bronx Expressway to the Throgs Neck Bridge, to the Cross Island Parkway, to the Long Island Expressway, and follow the same directions as below. From midtown Manhattan, take the Midtown Tunnel to the Long Island Expressway east to exit 39 North (Guinea Woods Road), to Route 25A (also called Northern Boulevard). Turn right on Route 25A, pass C. W. Post College, and make a left on Wolver Hollow Road (Route 4). Planting Fields Road will be a right turn about 2.5 miles away, and the entrance is on the right.

An arboretum is not just a collection of trees. Planting Fields is a horticultural center for people who enjoy every sort of growing thing; there are greenhouses, plant collections, a wildflower walk, majestic trees, nature trails, sweeping lawns, a dwarf conifer garden, and in springtime a marvelous profusion of azaleas. In various seasons the 409-acre estate offers just about every sort of plant-life environment: about 160 acres are developed, and the rest is kept as a natural habitat of fields and woods. For this reason the most varied interests in growing or planting rare trees, herbs, or unusual plants can be satisfied. And if you just want a nice place to walk, the Planting Fields Arboretum is a simply beautiful place to wander.

This was once the private estate of William Robertson Coe. His home, Coe Hall, an elegant example of Elizabethan-style architecture, is occasionally used for concerts, other cultural events, and school activities. The grounds, which are now under the jurisdiction of the Long Island State Park Commission, are meticulously kept (in the developed section), with changing displays and identifying tags on trees, shrubbery, and flower beds. The wilder part is crisscrossed with trails. All sorts of courses in horticulture, painting, photography, and ecology are offered at the arboretum, as are guided tours of the green-houses and grounds, but you can also just go and wander about on your own. A brochure is offered at the headquarters, describing over 7,500 specimens in the Herbarium. A self-guided tour booklet and map are also available.

While the arboretum is open year-round, you should phone (516–922–9200 or 922–8600) for definite information on what you will see when you get there. Planting Fields is open daily from 10:00 A.M. to 5:00 P.M. mid-April through October, and until 4:30 P.M. November through mid-April. A small admission fee is charged except during weekdays in winter, when it is free; children under twelve are always free. We rec-ommend this walk for people of all ages. Children will find plenty to interest them, from natural to cultivated areas and perhaps their first greenhouse. There are many quite flat areas, though there are some longish distances from one thing to the next. But you'll enjoy even a short walk in these flower-ing, sweet-smelling acres. There are no refreshments, nor is picnicking allowed.

The Walk

The arboretum is divided into several sections. You can plan to "do" them all, or focus on separate parts. Here is what you can see outdoors: The grounds have majestic trees, many of which are the largest of their kind on Long Island. You'll find lindens, tulip trees, cedars-of-Lebanon, beech, elms, and Sargent weep-ing hemlocks, among many others.

There are azaleas and rhododendrons galore. Some 600 plants make up this collection, which is famous throughout the East.

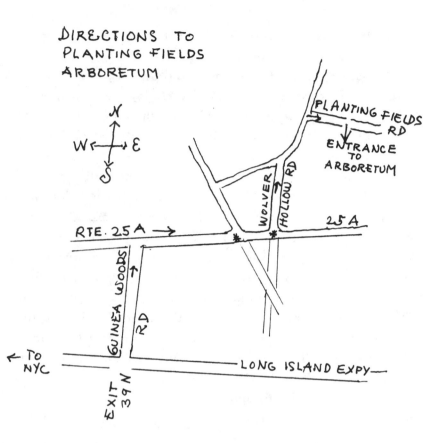

DIRECTIONS TO
PLANTING FIELDS
ARBORETUM

N
W · E
S

PLANTING FIELDS
RD
ENTRANCE
TO
ARBORETUM

WOLVER
HOLLOW RD

RTE. 25 A →   25 A

GUINEA WOODS
RD

← TO
NYC   LONG ISLAND EXPY

EXIT 39 N

(Late April or early May is a good time to visit for this reason.) In spring you'll also see daffodils, magnolias, forsythia, weeping cherries, dogwoods, flowering crab apples, lilacs, and wisterias. Summertime finds the grounds filled with blooming mountain laurel and changing annual border flowers. Each season has its beauties at the arboretum; in fall chrysanthemums and franklinia are set off by the brilliant foliage.

The five-acre Synoptic Garden, a specialty here, is an unusual arrangement of ornamental shrubs and small trees. The plants are alphabetically arranged, each identified with a label describing its family, country of origin, and botanical and common names. The Dwarf Conifer Garden is of particular interest to

69

those with small gardens themselves; it features a wide range of miniature, or dwarf, plants and bulbs.

The nature trails, on the other hand, are just as rough and natural as the gardens are manicured. Enjoy the woodsy walks and the birds you spot as you stroll. You should get the map at the desk before leaving the parking area, for this is an extensive place.

The indoor greenhouses, always an elegant addition to an estate, are just as you would expect: filled with bright colors and pretty patterns, these are familiar, rather than exotic, plants. Winter displays include poinsettias, cyclamen, and camellias. March brings the English spring garden and a profusion of orchids. In April an Easter display and cactus plants are featured, and in May geraniums of different types are exhibited. The summer finds the greenhouses filled with bedding plants such as begonias and impatiens, and in autumn chrysanthemums and orchids are shown. Occasional displays feature oddities such as banana and coffee plants.

It is, of course, the grounds that make this trip special, but a visit to the greenhouses is a nice way to complete your outing.

After the Walk

The village of Oyster Bay is a charming little community, once a whaling town. Many of the original buildings still exist. You can visit a number of historic houses there and poke into the boutiques and restaurants that line the short Main Street area.

Not far away is Sagamore Hill, Teddy Roosevelt's extraordinary summer home and the nearby gardens (if you haven't had your fill of garden walks). See Outing 16 for details about Sagamore Hill.

16 | Teddy Roosevelt's Sagamore Hill
Oyster Bay

How to Get There: From uptown Manhattan, take the Cross Bronx Expressway to the Throgs Neck Bridge, to the Cross Island Parkway, to the Long Island Expressway east, to exit 41 north. Take Route 106 north to Oyster Bay, turn right at the third traffic light, and follow signs to Sagamore Hill on Cove Neck Road. (The site is well marked.) From midtown Manhattan, take the Midtown Tunnel to the Long Island Expressway and follow the same directions as above.

Sagamore Hill is neither a mansion nor a grand reminder of long-gone elegance. It is a large but unpretentious and entirely charming family home high above a cove at Oyster Bay, and it is both historically and scenically delightful. There are lots to look at, from the rambling, spacious house and veranda, to the historical museum down the garden path, to a magnificent view in all directions. The atmosphere is quiet and reminiscent; you get quite a feeling of Teddy Roosevelt as you wander through the house and examine the wild game heads and skins on the walls, the mementoes of travel, and the dark paneled rooms, all with vistas of the sea. At the Old Orchard Museum you'll find historic exhibits relating to Teddy's political career, his personal life, and to the six Roosevelt children. A visit to Sagamore Hill can also include driving about a mile to his grave site, which adjoins a museum, formal gardens, and a bird sanctuary administered by the Audubon Society.

Sagamore Hill was built by Roosevelt during 1884 and 1885, after the death of his first wife. When it was completed entirely to his specifications ("I wished a big piazza," he wrote, "where

we could sit in rocking chairs and look at the sunset . . ."), he moved in with his sister Anna and his small daughter, Alice. Soon afterward he remarried; three of his six children were born at Sagamore Hill. Here T.R. spent the rest of his life, entertaining political and international guests, and enjoying his family until his death in 1919. "After all," he wrote, "fond as I am of the White House and much though I have appreciated these years in it, there isn't any place in the world like home—like Sagamore Hill, where things are our own, with our own associations."

For some thirty years Sagamore Hill was home to the Roosevelts, a large and cheerful family of endless interest to the public. Newspapers maintained a vigil at Sagamore Hill, chronicling the family's outdoor pastimes; T.R. could frequently be seen playing with his children, hiking, swimming, and riding horseback across his property. What he described as "the joy of life" was part of his national image of family man, sportsman, and statesman. Some of that feeling is evident to the visitor today. It is not hard to imagine the Roosevelt family of the turn of the century bustling through these comfortable rooms and enjoying the expansive veranda.

We suggest that you visit Sagamore Hill and the surrounding sites during the week, if you can. A popular spot, it gets a heavy dose of tourists, particularly at vacation times. All of the buildings are open year-round (closed on major holidays) from 10:00 A.M. to 4:00 P.M.; tours on the hour. There is a small admission charge. The trails at the bird sanctuary are open from 2:00 to 5:00 P.M. daily. There are no refreshments at any of the sites. Picnicking is not allowed, but nearby Oyster Bay has many eating places.

This is a good outing for walkers of all levels, as it is flat and has easy footing, but there are stairs.

For further information on Sagamore Hill, call (516) 922–4447.

The Walk

Sagamore Hill is a twenty-three room Victorian house made of frame and brick. The downstairs includes a large center hall, a library that served as T.R.'s office, Mrs. Roosevelt's drawing room, a dining room, kitchen, and a spacious north room added in 1905. This room in particular reflects T.R.'s personality; here you'll see the hunting trophies, books, flags, paintings, and mementoes of his life. On the second floor are the charming bedrooms and the nursery, and don't miss the giant porcelain bathtub! On the top floor you'll find the gun room, housing T.R.'s collection of hunting arms, though he also used it to entertain his friends in privacy. There are rooms for cooks and maids, a sewing room, and a schoolroom. Also of interest is the president's bedroom as it looked in his pre-Harvard days. Throughout you'll notice bulging bookcases, paintings, and memorabilia that are all of interest.

Outdoors you'll find landscaped gardens, the Roosevelt family pet cemetery, and a path to the Old Orchard Museum. Opened to the public in 1966, the museum contains three permanent exhibits, a gallery, a projection room, and a large collection of Roosevelt memorabilia, including a number of documentaries and motion pictures about T.R. and the family. T.R.'s son built the house called Old Orchard in 1938; in 1960 it was added to the Sagamore Hill National Historic Site.

You can return to your car after visiting these two sites and the grounds, and drive down the hill for about a mile to the Theodore Roosevelt Sanctuary. Here you'll find a series of bird-watching trails, some formal gardens, and T.R.'s grave. The sanctuary also has exhibits, bird attracting devices, and plantings. You can have guided tours, too, by calling (516) 922–3200.

After the Walk

This part of the North Shore is strikingly beautiful, and any one of the necks jutting out into Long Island Sound has great views, or a beach or harbor to explore. There are also several pleasant towns to wander through, including Cold Spring Harbor and Northport. We suggest exploring Oyster Bay, which has other interesting sites, including Raynham Hall, a 1740s house that contained the British headquarters during the Revolutionary War (call 516–922–6808 for information), and Planting Fields Arboretum (see Outing 15). Not far away is the Vanderbilt Mansion (see Outing 14), if you want to see two quite dissimilar estates in one day.

17 | A Breakwater and Beach Walk on the Sound

Eatons Neck

How to Get There: From uptown Manhattan, take the Cross Bronx Expressway to the Throgs Neck Bridge, to the Cross Island Parkway, to the Long Island Expressway east to exit 51, which is Route 231. Go north on Route 231, passing the Northern State Parkway intersection. At Route 25 (Jericho Turnpike) get on Route 10, which will take you into Northport. To reach Eatons Neck, take Ocean Avenue, then Asharoken Road to Eatons Neck Road to the end. From midtown Manhattan take the Midtown Tunnel to the Long Island Expressway and follow the same directions as above.

Anyone who has spent time on the seacoast remembers the fun of hopping, running, or strolling on the long breakwaters that stretch into the harbors of so many New England towns. We were happy to discover one that is only about an hour from the city, and on a lovely stretch of pebbly beach, too. The breakwater on this oddly shaped beach is really on the neck of a neck: Eatons Neck is a peninsula that stretches out into the waters of Long Island Sound north of Northport, and the beach itself is a long, skinny strip of sand and rocks that juts out from the end of it. When we visited (not in summer) there were one or two fishermen casting from the rocks, and one solitary stroller with his dog. The air was fresh and salty, the beach filled with wonderful pebbles of a hundred hues, and the breakwater quite a challenge.

The stroller informed us that people enjoy a sport here that they call "bouldering." It consists of jumping from the top of one giant stone to the next, despite spaces, odd surfaces, and pointed rocks. We can't give you a competitive time to complete

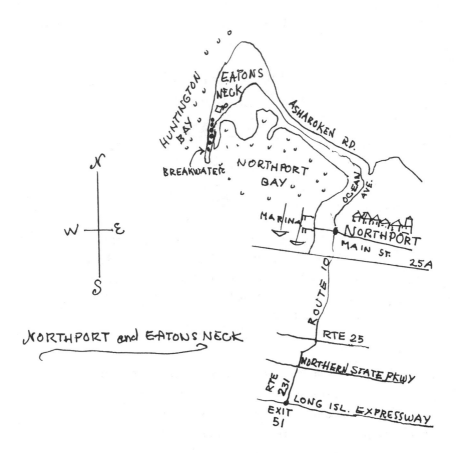

NORTHPORT and EATONS NECK

your breakwater bouldering, but we do recommend that you be careful. Enjoy yourself on as much of the long breakwater as you can do, and then set off to walk on the beach alongside and beyond the rest of the way.

The beach itself is a typical North Shore strand, densely covered with pebbles, occasional shells, and driftwood. When we walked it in the fall and spring, we found it pleasantly empty of trash. The beachcomber can pick up little rose-quartz stones, skipping stones, irregularly shaped driftwood, and the usual flotsam and jetsam.

In order to reach this beach, you will have driven through an unusually charming North Shore village called Northport. We recommend that you return to it after you've enjoyed the beach walk, and explore the bustling marina and main street.

Northport, which was once known as Cowharbor, was founded in 1656. It has had a flourishing history as a ship-building and fishing village, and then as a summer resort for New Yorkers at the turn of the twentieth century. The harbor, which still supports crabbing and oystering, is a busy recreational boaters' haven, and the charming town green, with its circular bandstand and paths leading to the wooden wharf, will remind you of an old—fashioned seaside setting from earlier days. The main street shops cater to visiting boaters, as well as to the recently arrived residents who have spruced up the many original and antique houses. There are restaurants and ice-cream parlors and boutiques galore, but the town has not succumbed to commercial cuteness and is a very pleasant place to stroll. If you like looking at old houses of various architectural styles, don't miss Bayview, the waterfront street of nineteenth century homes.

We do not recommend this outing in midsummer, unless you pick a rainy day or want to swim and don't mind crowds of people. If you go early in the morning or toward evening, you'll see a good variety of birds at the tip of the neck, which was once a wildlife preserve.

It is windy on the neck, so bundle up. Anyone planning to do the breakwater should wear sneakers. You can buy all the refreshments you'd ever want in Northport, but the beach is a good spot for a picnic, too. If you're a birder, bring binoculars. Many waterfowl and migrating birds like this remote tip of land.

The sand spit itself is totally flat and the sand is not soft, so any walker of any age can enjoy it. The breakwater is hard going and only for the most fit, but this is a good hike for a family to do together, as the energetic ones can hop along the rocks, while the more sedate can walk beside them.

The Walk

Leave your car in the lot at the end of Eatons Neck Road, where you will see the boat launching area and a small brick building. Walk straight out toward the beach. The breakwater begins about 0.25 mile out into the beach. Off-season you'll be strolling along a quite deserted stretch, or hopping the odd-shaped rocks of the breakwater that protects the bay harbor from storm and tide. From the end of the breakwater you can keep going farther and farther from the village and out to the lonely tip of sand, pebbles, and seagulls. The distances are not great: The entire walk is perhaps 2 miles (but don't forget you have to go back, too). The breakwater is about 0.5 to 0.75 mile of that 2 miles.

After the Walk

We have already suggested that you explore the marina and village of Northport. You can also visit several nearby attractions: the Vanderbilt Mansion (see Outing 14); Caumsett (see Outing 13); or start back toward New York and stop at Teddy Roosevelt's wonderful Sagamore Hill (see Outing 16).

The Hudson Valley (East)

18 | Over and Under a Dam

The New Croton Dam, Cortland

How to Get There: From midtown Manhattan, take the Henry Hudson Parkway north and continue on the Saw Mill River Parkway. Follow the signs for Route 9 north and Tarrytown. Continue on Route 9 north past North Tarrytown, Scarborough, and Ossining. You'll see a sign for Croton-on-Hudson. Take the second exit, following the signs for Route 129. Stay on Route 129 for about 4 miles. The entrance to Croton Gorge Park is on your right. You can either enter the park, cross the wooden bridge, and leave your car there; or, continue on Route 129 for about 0.3 mile, take Croton Dam Road on your right, and park your car just before reaching the dam.

It's been hailed as the eighth wonder of the world, the most beautiful of all dams, the one with the most impressive masonry work. It's been praised, sung about, immortalized in verse and on canvas, and made into a National Historic Site. It's been walked over and photographed. The Croton Dam, majestically situated high amid the rolling Westchester hills, continues to impress the visitor. Crossing it on foot and then walking down into the park below—the undeveloped Croton Gorge Park—to get another good view of it, makes for an unusual and interesting outing.

A bit of history should be kept in mind at this spectacular site. The dam—called the New Croton Dam to distinguish it from its predecessor—supplies much of New York City's water, some 400 million gallons out of the almost 2 billion gallons the city needs daily. During the 1830s, after New York City was devastated by cholera and fire, the city planners realized that the city's growing population could no longer rely on the existing

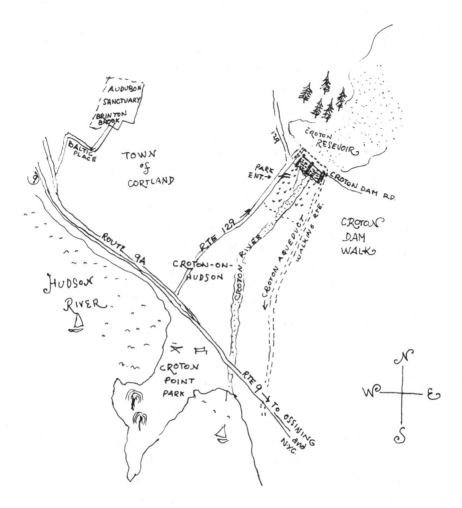

water supply (from local springs and wells) and that a new dam and aqueduct would have to be built to bring in more water. The Croton River, with its various branches and abundant, pure, and wholesome water, seemed a good choice for the creation of these waterworks.

The first dam, worked on by Irish laborers fleeing the potato famine, was completed in 1842. However, some years later it became apparent that a new dam would have to be built to accommodate the ever-expanding city. After many preliminary studies, the northern end of the Croton River watershed was chosen for a high masonry dam, and work on the project was finally begun in 1892. Highways, homes, and hotels had to be relocated to build roads, bridges, and superstructures. Italian laborers with expertise in stone masonry were imported from southern Italy and Sicily. Unfortunately, a variety of engineering mishaps and labor unrest due to the miserable conditions caused the work to drag on. On April 1, 1900, the workers staged a huge wildcat strike. They came roaring down the hill, brandishing knives and threatening to blow up the dam. The Westchester National Guard and Teddy Roosevelt's Rough Riders were called in to quell the riot.

After further delays, the final stone of the dam was laid on December 15, 1906, and the dam officially opened in January 1907 amid great celebration. Instead of the intended five years and $4 million, it took almost fifteen years to build and cost almost $12 million. At 297 feet high and 2,168 feet long, it was the largest dam in the world at that time. The amount of masonry used to build it was said to be equal to that used in building the Great Pyramid of Cheops!

On this trip, we recommend you take binoculars, and a sketch pad or camera to record the scenery on both sides of the dam. There are no designated picnic spots or public facilities either in the park or on the Old Croton Aqueduct trail nearby, but opportunities for picnicking are not lacking. If you intend to make this a longer walk, bring drinking water and wear solid shoes.

Although the actual crossing of the dam is hardly rigorous (and is fairly short), the walk up and down and around it is more tiring. Those who don't like hills might choose to limit their walk accordingly. If you decide to venture forth on the Old Croton Aqueduct pathway, you'll find the going easy and basically flat. This is an all-season walk. If you plan to continue on the Old Croton Aqueduct trail, arrange for transportation somewhere along this lengthy route. Croton Gorge Park is never crowded because of its lack of facilities (we were there on a Labor Day weekend and saw only a couple of people).

To take the full Old Croton Aqueduct walk, obtain the walk directory from New York State Parks, Taconic Region, Staatsburg, NY 12580, or call (914) 693–5259.

The Walk

Either park your car inside Croton Gorge Park (no fee) and begin your walk from there, or drive directly to the dam, leaving your car by the side of the road. If you've chosen the first option, walk across a picturesque wooden bridge and up through the park entrance, turning right onto Route 129 and going up the hill for a short distance. Go right at Croton Dam Road and proceed to the dam.

Crossing the dam won't take very long—it's only about 0.3 mile—but you'll want to stop and enjoy the views on both sides. On your right you can admire the rolling hills of the Croton River Valley. The meandering river is not very visible because of the dense woodlands surrounding it, but you can observe the reservoir water rushing through the dam's spillway into it. (Unfortunately, you can also see junk that people have thrown down from the dam walkway!) On the reservoir side—the left as you walk across the dam—you see a peaceful, large lake with an occasional fisherman's rowboat (fishing is allowed only with permit). From here you can admire the masonry that has been so praised. You'll be awestruck by the impressive engineering feat this dam represents.

After you have crossed the dam, you'll see a path (with two large rocks in front) immediately to the right. This marks the beginning of the Old Croton Aqueduct trail, which goes all the way to 173rd Street in upper Manhattan, some 32 miles, crossing woodlands, meadows, estates, abandoned farms, and suburbs. The Old

Croton Aqueduct, finished in the 1840s along with the Old Croton Dam, was taken out of service to New York City in 1955 and has since been used by walkers, joggers, bikers, equestrians, and cyclists. You might choose to walk along this trail for whatever distance you feel up to, remembering that you'll have to retrace your steps. This path is a naturalist's delight. In spring blooming dogwood, mountain laurel, and other shrubs proliferate. In summer you can pick blackberries. There are wooded areas of pine, oak, hemlock, and mulberry where you might spot a deer, raccoon, or rabbit. Birders can observe cardinals, red-winged blackbirds, robins, crows, and pheasants.

If your time is limited, start on this trail, walk for a few moments, then leave the trail, turning right and going down a fairly steep grassy slope into Croton Gorge Park. (There is no actual path leading you to the park, only the evidence of others who have made their own trail.) Walk across the meadow to the dam and view it from this new perspective. You can especially appreciate the details of stonework from this angle. Then walk along the river for a while, if you are willing to make your own way over rocks and through woods. There are no trails in this park; it is completely undeveloped, with the exception of the small parking area and a modest children's playground off to the side.

After the Walk

We have several suggestions, depending on your time and energy level. You can combine this outing with Outing 22. The aqueduct goes through Rockefeller State Park Preserve, less than 10 miles south.

A pleasant drive along the reservoir (Croton Lake) is enjoyable—particularly in fall with the spectacular foliage. Drive across the dam and continue on the road (Croton Lake Road) all the way around. It becomes a dirt road, but is fairly wide, scenic, and uncrowded. You pass by two bridges; cross at the third (for a longer drive, keep going straight), and get back onto Route 129. The lake is to your left at all times. Eventually you will cross another bridge over the lake. This circular drive is about 9 miles long.

Croton Point Park is an especially scenic spot and worth seeing, if only to admire its spectacular situation on the Hudson. Unlike Croton Gorge Park, this is a somewhat developed area with playing fields, a family campground (off to the side), picnic tables at water's edge, a playground, and a small bathing beach—if you care to swim in the Hudson. Situated on a dramatic point that juts out into the river, it commands great views of the entire region on all sides: Haverstraw and Hook Mountain lie directly across; historic Tarrytown lighthouse, the Tappan Zee Bridge, and the New York City skyline can be seen to the far south on a clear day. On the other side of this peninsula lies Croton Bay, with its surrounding tidal marsh where loons, egrets, and cormorants live. There is good fishing along the banks of the river because of the rich marsh habitat. Fishermen we talked to said they hoped to catch striped bass, perch, Atlantic sturgeon, or weakfish. The park has great expanses of grassy fields with willows and locust trees and a nearby conifer forest. It is open daily from 8:00 A.M. to dusk, and there is a small fee for parking. Pets are not allowed.

The Audubon Sanctuary at Brinton Brook northwest of the dam is also a nice spot for birding.

19 | Sleepy Hollow Cemetery

Tarrytown

How to Get There: From midtown Manhattan, east side take F.D.R. Drive to the Major Deegan Expressway north, which becomes the New York State Thruway. Exit at Route 9, just before the Tappan Zee Bridge (exit 9) at Tarrytown. Go north on Route 9, which is Broadway, through Tarrytown; the cemetery is on your right. From midtown Manhattan, west side, take the Henry Hudson Parkway, which becomes the Saw Mill River Parkway, to the New York State Thruway and follow the directions above.

Sleepy Hollow Cemetery is a rare graveyard—neither dismal nor unattractive. Its rolling terrain and giant trees shelter the graves of all sorts of people, from early Dutch settlers of this Hudson River area, to the great robber barons and philanthropists of the nineteenth century, to the most famous of the area's native sons, Washington Irving, whose lovely home, Sunnyside, is nearby.

The walks through this cemetery are as long or as short as you wish to make them; at every turn you'll come across lovely vistas, interesting markers, and even a gurgling river with a wooden bridge. An attendant at the main gate will give you a map outlining (very roughly indeed) where to locate the most famous graves. But if you enjoy this type of walk, you'll find yourself wandering more or less at random, among the giant mausoleums of the late nineteenth century, the old sandstone markers of the early Dutch and English settlers, and the charming iron-fenced plots of early families.

While strolling through a cemetery or making grave rubbings may be an acquired taste, we found this particular site

A WALK THROUGH SLEEPY HOLLOW CEMETERY

LOOK FOR:
1. OLD CHURCH YARD
   and
   OLD DUTCH CHURCH
2. WASHINGTON IRVING'S GRAVE
3. REVOLUTIONARY WAR MONUMENT
4. DELAVAN MONUMENT
5. ANDREW CARNEGIE'S GRAVE
6. SAMUEL GOMPERS'S GRAVE
7. WILLIAM ROCKEFELLER'S MAUSOLEUM

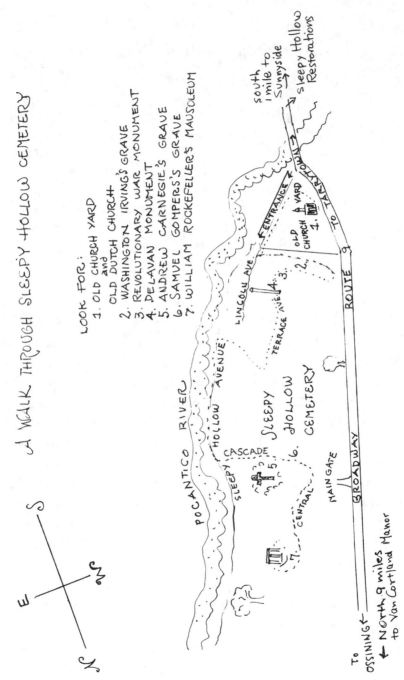

filled with interest—historical, scenic, and visual, for many of the monuments are quite extraordinary. There are Greek Revival mausoleums, obelisks and columns surmounted with flying angels, as well as hundreds of more common markers. The cemetery is uncrowded and quite large, so you can walk about at will, meeting, as we did, only gardeners carefully tending the flowering shrubbery and grassy hillsides. Washington Irving called the area "a sequestered glen . . . one of the quietest places in the whole world . . ." Fortunately, his words still seem true.

We recommend this outing to those with an interest in history and a taste for this special kind of walk. (Most probably this group will not include children.) The trek is somewhat hilly and can be very long, depending on where you park and how far you wish to go, but for the moderately fit visitor, it's an easy outing. The walkways are mostly soft, though some are paved. You should not bring pets or radios or other noise-makers, as there is a sense of silence you wouldn't want to disturb. If you like making grave rubbings, by all means bring paper and the soft crayon sold at most art supply stores especially for this purpose. (Several good monuments for rubbings are identified below.)

Sleepy Hollow Cemetery is open daily from 8:30 A.M. to 4:30 P.M. year-round. It is particularly pretty in spring and fall, but there is no reason you shouldn't visit on a coolish summer day. The Old Dutch Church, however, is open only on Sundays (when you can also take a tour).

The Walk

The Old Dutch Church stands at one end of the cemetery, surrounded by the oldest graves. The rushing little river, the Pocantico, is crossed by Irving's "Headless Horseman Bridge" just below. The rest of the cemetery's oldest sections lie between

Broadway (Route 9) and the river; across the little river is a newer (and less interesting) section.

You can park either near the Old Dutch Church or within the cemetery along one of the winding roads, and begin your walk either at the Old Church (as shown on our map) or at the main gate, where you pick up your map from the office. (The map is almost illegible, but it might help you find your way from one walkway to the next.)

If you start at the church (1 on our map), take a look first at this very old landmark. It was built by Frederick Philipse (see Philipsburg Manor described below) in 1697 or 1699 for his family and the tenants of the manor house. The cupola contains the original bell, making it more than 300 years old. There are not many landmarks in our country of that antiquity. The legend reads "If God be for us, who can be against us?" Both Philipse and his wife, Catherine Van Cortland (see Van Cortland Manor below), are buried beneath the chancel of the church. If you can't get in, peak through the windows at the simple and charming architecture.

The graves in the churchyard are among the oldest at Sleepy Hollow. Here you'll see the same names many times, with markers bearing the traditional weeping willow design. (Most are too decayed for grave rubbings, though one or two have clear-cut carving.)

Next, seek out Washington Irving's fenced-in family plot. Try walking northward on Lincoln Avenue, to Crane, to Paulding. Irving's grave (2) is in a charming little garden with about fifty family graves surrounding it. There is a giant tree sheltering them all, and a wrought-iron gate and fence encircling both tree and graves. Irving, author of some of America's best-loved classics ("The Legend of Sleepy Hollow" among them), was both an author and diplomat. He lived from 1783 to 1859. His grave and garden around it seem appropriately old and charming.

If you walk on, following the winding road (unnamed), you'll come to the Revolutionary War monument (3), which is unremarkable except for its beautiful hillside location with a distant view. Directly behind it is the Delavan monument (4), a strikingly tall column with a figure high atop. David Delavan (1757–1835) is buried here, surrounded with giant sculpted angels. It is a site worth noticing. Just behind it, in the Hawes plot, is a good grave rubbing monument with a traditional willow design. It might say "Cornelia Amy," but it's hard to read.

As you walk between the locusts and cypresses and evergreen trees, you'll pass some extraordinary mausoleums and chapels, built in a variety of classical and romantic styles. Turn down toward the river for a walk along its rippling banks on Sleepy Hollow Avenue. Eventually you'll come to another road up the hill (away from the river) called Cascade Avenue.

If you make your way steadily up and follow the paths, you'll come to two more interesting graves: first, and somewhat hidden from the walkway, is the Celtic cross marking the grave of Andrew Carnegie. Carnegie (5), who lived from 1835 to 1919, was the great industrialist (founder of Carnegie Steel) and philanthropist who built Carnegie Hall and many public libraries, and gave away some $350 million for public institutions. His grave is in a small circular garden, reached from the walkway by a short stone path. It is in the style of a fine Celtic cross with many carved markings, and it is beautifully set and neither ostentatious nor grand.

Just across the roadway is the grave of Samuel Gompers (6), the labor leader and first president of the American Federation of Labor. Gompers, who died in 1924, has a distinctly unfancy grave marker, placed there by the union.

Finally, make your way up to the crest of a hill where you'll find the huge mausoleum of William Rockefeller (7). This massive neoclassical building has Ionic columns and inscribed walls like a public institution; other members of the Rockefeller family are also buried around it. It sits, in great splendor, in a circular space with a giant hedge surrounding it. William Rockefeller (1841–1922) was a brother and associate of John D. and a co-developer of Standard Oil.

You can continue wandering on your own, of course. Among the other graves of interest are those of Mark Hellinger, for whom a Broadway theater was named; Major Bowes, the 1940s radio personality; and Walter Chrysler, the American auto industrialist. However, you might find, as we did, that many of the most interesting graves are those bearing unfamiliar names.

After the Walk

The entire Tarrytown region is filled with interesting historic sites, most in some way related to the legendary Sleepy Hollow. Here are some of the side visits you might want to take after your cemetery walk.

Sleepy Hollow Restorations is a collection of beautifully restored homes, all furnished in period antiques. You'll get a taste of what life was once like in the Hudson River Valley. Among the restored buildings are: Sunnyside, Washington Irving's charming home, still maintained in his style, with desk, wood stove, etc. Here you can take a tour and stroll through the gardens to the banks of the Hudson. Van Cortland Manor, the home of one of the Hudson Valley's earliest prominent families, is a fine example of architecture of the Dutch period, with its sweeping staircase, porch, and graceful garden. There are demonstrations of manor life (a la Williamsburg), including colonial crafts. Finally, there's a Philipsburg Manor, a fine job of restoration that returns an entire manor—from farmhouse to garden to mills—to its original appearance, between 1720 and 1750. It is most appealing, with bare floors, whitewashed walls, and simple charm.

In our opinion, the entire restoration is slightly marred by period costumes on the guides, tours, educational films, and other "restoration-itis," apparently aimed at schoolchildren. However, if you go to Tarrytown, Sunnyside alone is well worth the visit. The restorations are open from 10:00 A.M. to 5:00 P.M. daily, closed major holidays and Tuesdays in winter. Call (914) 631–8200 for specific information, as well as admission prices, which vary according to the number of places you visit.

Lyndhurst, a Gothic Revival castle and the home of Jay Gould the financier, is also just down the street from the cemetery in Tarrytown (at 635 South Broadway). This rather odd nineteenth-century palace overlooking the Hudson has a treasure trove of furniture, decorations, Tiffany glass, silver, rugs, fine paintings, and trompe l'oeil designs.

A real find among all of this history is the small Union Church just up the road from Tarrytown in Pocantico Hills. Here, nestled in the pretty village where the palatial Rockefeller estate is located, is a lovely ivy-covered church housing stained-glass windows by Marc Chagall and a wonderful rose window by Henri Matisse. Seven of these stunning windows, mostly memorials to various members of the Rockefeller family, are devoted to Old Testament prophets and are amazingly like Chagall's paintings with their brilliant colors and biblical designs. Admission is by donation. To reach the church, turn up the hill (away from the river) at the center of Tarrytown on Route 448 and follow the winding road to Pocantico Hills. The church is open Monday, Wednesday, Thursday, and Friday, 11:00 A.M. to 5:00 P.M.; Saturday, 10:00 A.M. to 5:00 P.M.; Sunday, 2:00 P.M. to 5:00 P.M.

20 | A Hemlock Woodland Gorge

Mianus River Gorge Wildlife Refuge and Botanical Preserve, Westchester County

How to Get There: From uptown Manhattan, take the Major Deegan Expressway, which becomes the New York State Thruway, north to the Cross County Parkway. Go east to the Hutchinson River Parkway to Interstate 684 north. Exit at Route 22 north and follow signs for Bedford Village. From the center of the village, follow the signs for Route 172. Turn right at Long Ridge Road (where you will also see a sign for Stamford, Connecticut), continue for about a mile, turn right on Millers Mill Road, then left on Mianus River Road. The gorge is a half mile down the road on your left.

An excursion to the Mianus River Gorge Wildlife Refuge and Botanical Preserve is ideal if you are seeking an unspoiled wilderness in relatively close proximity to New York City. Located less than 40 miles northeast of Manhattan in a rural section of Westchester County, the park includes about 450 acres of pristine woodland, mostly hemlock and beech, along the banks and gorge of the Mianus River. The gorge is a deep ravine that was carved out by a great sheet of ice some 10,000 or more years ago. The name of the river comes from Myanos, a local Indian chief the white settlers met when they first arrived in the seventeenth century.

This is an inviting spot for a quiet walk in a natural and tranquil sylvan setting. The only sounds you hear are those of birds (there are more than 150 species), or the rushing river in the ravine, or a nearby gurgling brook. There are 5 miles of foot trails that go up and down over hilly terrain, amid a rich variety of plant and animal life. The dense, dark evergreen forest

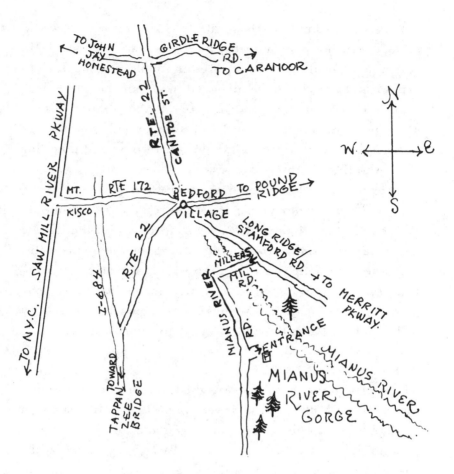

alternates with leafy, airy woodlands of maples, beeches, tulip trees, and dogwoods, so that you go in and out of shadows, with varying degrees of sunlight filtering through the foliage.

The conservation-minded founders of the preserve decided not to provide outdoor recreation in a traditional park setting with playing fields and picnic facilities. In fact, there are a number of restrictions, which no doubt account for the fact that the preserve is uncrowded and without the usual distractions: no fires, smoking, dogs (even on leashes), picnics, hunting, boating, or camping.

A walk in this preserve is wonderful for urban dwellers who seldom have the opportunity to experience nature firsthand. We recommend it also for adventuresome children who love to explore and who should be intrigued by an enormous hemlock reputed to be more than 300 years old. Although the trails are quite hilly, they are not too difficult to manage if you proceed at a leisurely pace. However, we do not recommend them for those who find climbing arduous.

The preserve is closed from December 1 to April 1. Late spring is a wonderful time to go, particularly if you are partial to wild-flowers; summer is pleasant, with warm breezes on the hillside above the gorge; and, of course, the autumn trees are resplendent. We suggest you equip yourself with sturdy walking shoes, since the trails can be fairly rugged, though well-maintained. Save your picnic for after your visit to Mianus Gorge. Open daily from 8:30 A.M. to 5:00 P.M. Call (914) 234–3455 for more information.

The Walk

The approach to the preserve sets the tone for what is to come. From Millers Mill Road you drive along Miller's Mill Dam with its impressive cascade, bearing to the left and following discreet signs to the entrance of the preserve. Park your car, and at the shelter pick up a trail map, which gives you a good description of where you are going. Basically you will be staying on one trail, which is marked in red going out and blue coming back. There are detours worth making along the way, all of which are indi-cated on the trail guide.

As you start on your walk, you are struck by the silence around you. After a moment you will see a small wooden bench on your right, slightly off the trail, with a view overlooking the beginning of the gorge. This bench, called the Lucy D.S. Adams Memorial Bench, was placed there for those who cannot walk the trails but want to enjoy this special environment.

You proceed over a soft carpet of pine needles, leaves, and mosses, always following the well-marked trail. You cross a charming little stone bridge over a brook with masses of ferns and beeches alongside. The path leads you up and down hills, with occasional views of the gorge below. About a half hour into the walk, you will come to a place where you make a sharp turn up a rather steep hill with random stone steps and gnarled tree roots. You are now on your way to the "Hemlock Cathedral," a twenty-acre site of tall, majestic trees atop a hill. This is a quiet place. The sunlight filtering through the trees creates the impression of the interior of a Gothic church. You then pass a beech grove and a wild ginger colony and will see a series of lovely old stone walls along the way that marked the boundaries between farms of long ago. A recommended detour is Hobby Hill Quarry, where mica, quartz, and feldspar were mined during the eighteenth century. We also suggest you take a few minutes and follow the signs for the reservoir view.

Havemeyer Falls, one of the main sights of the excursion, are finally reached after you go down a fairly rugged, rocky path that can be slippery with wet leaves and roots. Follow the sound of the falls as they cascade over the rocks, and you are there. This gentle waterfall may not be dramatic, but is a lovely spot to stop for a moment. If you follow the trail to the lookout point at the end, you will be rewarded with a fine view of the entire region, including the reservoir and gorge. Retrace your steps, following the blue markers back to your starting point. The entire walk (about 5 miles if you include the various detours) is no more than three hours, if taken at a leisurely pace. It's impossible to get lost, as everything is well marked.

After the Walk

Nearby Bedford Village is worth a short visit. Surrounded by elegant nineteenth-century frame houses that line the pleasant, shaded streets, it is clustered around a village green, like many traditional New England towns. Don't miss the charming Carpenter Gothic Presbyterian church and the eighteenth-century courthouse, now a small museum.

Caramoor, the impressive Mediterranean-style country estate of New York lawyer, banker, and art collector Walter Tower Rosen and his wife, Lucie Bigelow Dodge, is only a few minutes' drive from Bedford Village. (Follow Route 22 to the junction of Girdle Ridge Road, about 3.4 miles, where you'll see a small sign for Caramoor. Turn right and continue for about 0.5 mile, to the entrance of the estate.) Built in the 1930s to house the couple's extensive collection of European art and furniture, in 1970 it was opened to the public as a museum and center for music and the arts. It now hosts an internationally known music festival.

The house includes some fifty-five rooms (only nineteen of which are open for public viewing), all decorated in authentic period pieces from medieval monasteries of Spain and Italy, palaces and chateaux of France, and from China. It is built around a Moorish-style courtyard, where more intimate concerts are presented in the summer. During the winter, concerts are occasionally featured in the Music Room, an impressive 70-foot-long room with a magnificent carved ceiling from an Italian palace and splendid tapestries. Guided tours of the grounds and house (for a fee) are offered regularly Wednesday through Sunday and by appointment (you cannot visit the house on your own). Call (914) 232–5035 for information on the tours and concerts.

After you have visited the house, take a stroll through the lovely formal gardens, especially in spring when they are most impressive. Picnic tables for the public are scattered around a pleasant apple orchard, and you can wander past a grape arbor, fountain, cedar walk, gazebo, or farther afield into the acres of woodlands that enclose the grounds.

Also of interest is the extraordinary outdoor art collection belonging to Pepsico in nearby Purchase, New York. The Donald M. Kendall Sculpture Garden, set on 112 acres, features a great collection of twentieth-century sculpture, including notable works by such artists as Noguchi, Lipchitz, Moore, and Segal. A printed guide is available. For information (914) 253-2000.

21 | A Riverfront Village Stroll and/or a Mountain Climb Above

Cold Spring

How to Get There: From the George Washington Bridge, take the Palisades Interstate Parkway north, cross the Bear Mountain Bridge, then take Route 9D north along the river for 9 miles for a scenic route. From midtown Manhattan, take the Henry Hudson Parkway, which becomes the Saw Mill River Parkway, and then take Route 287 west to Route 9 north (at Tarrytown) to Route 9D north. From there follow the same directions as above. By public transportation, take the Metro-North from Grand Central Terminal to Cold Spring (212–532–4900).

The largely unspoiled Hudson River Valley remains one of our favorite areas for walking. A leisurely stroll in Cold Spring, a charming village on the east bank of the river across from West Point and about 50 miles north of the city, followed by a scenic climb up the Washburn Trail on nearby (less than a mile away) Mount Taurus, makes a fine excursion. The famed river views from the village dock, as well as from the mountain summit, are among the most spectacular in the Hudson Valley—especially in fall, when the surrounding hills are in their full foliage splendor.

Cold Spring is the kind of place that takes the visitor back to the days of the horse and buggy and such riverfront traditions as outdoor band concerts. The village is located in a scenic area that has retained its character from the days of the first Dutch explorers. The vistas of the river are unobstructed by factories or tall buildings. And Cold Spring's quaint Main Street is fun to amble along, with its antiques shops, a few very old houses, and the remains of a foundry dock at river's edge.

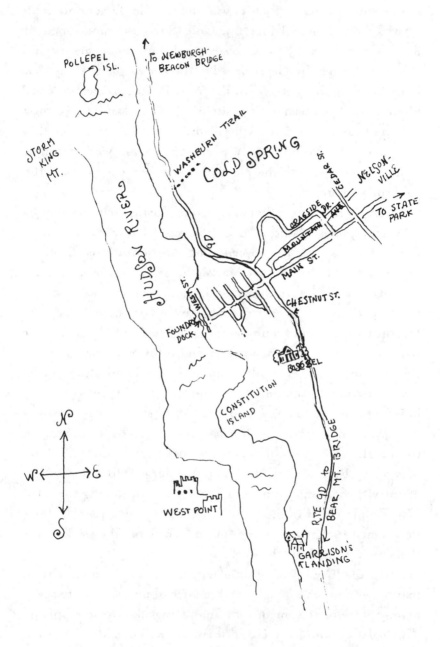

The history of the village of Cold Spring begins well before the Revolution. Its first settler was one Charles Davenport, who arrived from England in 1729. Cold Spring is mentioned in history accounts when George Washington's army passed through the nearby Garrison's Landing area on the day that Benedict Arnold's betrayal of the West Point fortifications was discovered. The encampment site of the army can be seen on a walking tour through the village, one of the several sites that date from the Revolutionary period. General Washington is thought to have given the place its name because he liked the cold spring water.

Several years after the war, Cold Spring was chosen by President James Madison to be the site of one of four iron foundries to supply the government with munitions. By 1820 the foundry at the foot of Market Street was completed and turning out its first cannons, and Cold Spring was well on its way to prosperity. The first locomotive engines, including the DeWitt Clinton, were built here, as were the first Hudson River steamboats and the first iron water mains for New York City and Boston. Among other products manufactured were stoves, bells, steam engines, machinery, and the cast-iron fronts of many buildings in the Soho section of Manhattan. Iron ore was brought to the foundry by river barge and then by train, and the town maintained its own fleet of sloops to carry finished prod-ucts away. By mid-century it was the largest foundry in the country, producing munitions for the North during the Civil War. Employment in the foundry was as high as 1,400. In 1865 President Lincoln visited the foundry to thank the workers for their help in winning the war.

After the Civil War, Daniel Adams Butterfield, a Union major general who fought at Fredericksburg and Gettysburg among other battles, made his home, Cragside, in Cold Spring. This palatial house (which, unfortunately, burned down a few years ago) once welcomed the grand duchess of Russia and other dignitaries who arrived at the dock and were escorted there. The Butterfields were prominent citizens whose bequests gave the village a library and hospital, in the tradition of leading citizens of small towns across America. Another noteworthy citizen of Cold Spring was George Pope Morris, founder and editor of the New York Mirror and several other newspapers, as well as a popular-song composer. Among his guests, who also arrived by Hudson River steamboat, were many literary figures, including Charles Dickens.

By the middle of the twentieth century, preservationists realized that Cold Spring's Main Street deserved saving. The architecture of the area is still much as it was more than a hundred years ago, and among the residents of the village are craftspeople and antiques enthusiasts who want to keep it that way.

Who would like this outing? The village walk will appeal to most anyone and is easy and pleasant. The climb up the Washburn Trail is, on the other hand, fairly steep and recommended only for the fittest hikers. Of course, you can do one and not the other, depending on your energy, time, and inclination. Both parts of the outing will be enhanced if you take along a pair of binoculars and perhaps a camera. There are several cozy cafes, so you need not bring your own food unless you would prefer a picnic on the shore of the river. Do bring some water and/or a snack for the hike on the trail.

We think that fall is the best time to visit Cold Spring and its surroundings. The town by then has settled down after the bustle of the tourist season, and, of course, the scenery is at its most glorious. However, if you like fireworks, you might want to come on the Fourth of July, when an impressive display can be viewed from the bandstand near the river. If your main interest is antiquing or shopping, remember that many antiques shops are somewhat erratic in their hours and tend to be open only during the latter part of the week and on weekends, especially during the off-season.

The Walk

The more interesting shops and old houses are found on a steep three-block stretch of Main Street that runs down to the river bandstand across from Storm King Mountain. Lining the street are shuttered frame buildings typical of nineteenth-century northern towns. From most merchants you can pick up a flier called "A Cold Spring Walking Tour," complete with map and all the major sites. Listed below are some of the places we encourage you to see.

The Chapel of Our Lady, one of the most charming in the entire Hudson Valley, is reached by going down Main Street toward the river. Turn left just before the railroad tracks and then left again. The chapel looks out over the river. Since its completion in 1833, this small and simple but dignified building with its four Doric columns has often been painted and drawn. The bandstand at the riverfront on West Street, the dock at the end of Market Street, the railroad station, and the George Washington plaque are all also worth a look.

The Gouverneur Kemble Warren Home at 8 Fair Street is an attractive Greek Revival building that can only be admired from the outside. If you're interested (and if you're there on the right day), stop by the Putnam County Historical Society Museum at 63 Chestnut Street. Here you'll see a portion of the original Foundry School built in the 1820s to educate youngsters apprenticing at the foundry. It is open to the public Tuesday and Wednesday, 10:00 A.M. to 2:00 P.M.; Thursday, 1:00 to 4:00 P.M.; Sunday, 2:00 to 5:00 P.M.; and by appointment (phone 845–265–4010).

The most charming (and popular) inn in the region, the Hudson House, is worth a brief visit or meal, if time permits.

Built in 1832 to house steamboat passengers, it has recently been tastefully renovated. Its location, right on the river next to a small pier where the steamboats docked, is special.

Of course, we recommend you walk along the river to enjoy the dramatic views. The Hudson is fairly narrow at this point, and you can clearly see the awe-inspiring and severe-looking Storm King Mountain looming across the water, as well as West Point farther down.

If you are a strong hiker and want to try the Washburn Trail, drive back up Main Street, turning left onto Route 9D. About 0.7 mile north is a clearing on the right, which will lead you to the trail. You can park a few feet in from the road at the foot of a driveway that used to lead to a now-abandoned stone quarry. Walk, bearing left immediately (and following an unmarked path) to a grassy slope and the first of the white blazes indicating the beginning of the trail. You will see a trail register attached to a tree.

The Washburn Trail, 2.3 miles of fairly rough climbing, starts from river level and goes 1,400 feet to the top of Mount Taurus. As you ascend you'll have great views of Storm King and the river valley to the west and south. After about 2 miles the trail meets an old carriage road, which you'll stay on, past the summit of Mount Taurus, to get more wonderful panoramic views north and west to Surprise Lake Valley, the Shawangunks, Breakneck Ridge, and even the Catskills! This trail ends when it meets the Notch Trail. You can either retrace your steps and go back down, or continue on the Notch Trail to Dairy Road, which will lead you back to Route 9D, about 0.25 mile north from where you started.

After the Walk

The surroundings of Cold Spring offer several sites that are worth a visit. Stonecrop Gardens, just outside Cold Spring, is a magnificent rock garden with rare plantings and waterfalls (see Outing 23).

Garrison's Landing is a tiny settlement with an impeccable nineteenth-century train station on the banks of the river. Its old-fashioned charm and unspoiled architecture made it the choice for the setting of the movie *Hello, Dolly!* in the 1960s. Don't miss St. Philips Church in the Highlands on Route 9D, a simple stone church with a pitched slate roof built in the 1840s, and St. Joseph's Catholic chapel, also a quaint building. Garrison's Landing is the site of many pottery studios and the Garrison Art Center displays some of these crafts. You can call them at (845) 424–3960, or take your chances and visit uninvited.

While in the area, visit Boscobel off Route 9D, a classical 1804 mansion built in the Federal style and beautifully preserved. You are invited to stroll through its lovely gardens and orangeries overlooking the Hudson. Inside there are rooms filled with antiques. Call(845) 265–3638 for information.

Nearby and also on Route 9D is Dick's (Dix) Castle, a typical eccentric's folly and giant Moorish-style curiosity modeled after the Alhambra in Spain.

Pollepel Island, which can be seen from Route 9D north of Cold Spring, contains the ruins of a Scottish-style castle (about to undergo restoration), built at the turn of the twentieth century. There is no access to the historic island now except when arranged through Bannerman Castle Trust (info@bannermancastle.org).

22 | A Reflective Lakeside Walk Only a Half Hour from the City

Rockefeller State Park Preserve, Tarrytown

How to Get There: From uptown Manhattan, take the Major Deegan Expressway north to the New York State Thruway to Route 9 (exit 9) northbound, through the villages of Tarrytown and North Tarrytown. Turn right on Route 117 and follow signs for the preserve. The entrance to the park is on the right.

This is a country walk surprisingly close to the city. The mixture of meadows, lakes and wooded paths (with occasional horseback riders appearing on the bridle paths) gives the walker the feeling of being on an English country estate. The grounds and paths are well tended, but not overdone, the natural beauty of a Hudson Valley landscape unspoiled, the lake clean and rippling. The preserve is indeed that—preserved for walking and enjoying the weather and feeding the ducks or observing nature. Despite its proximity to a bustling village and busy highways, once inside the preserve you'll find it hard to believe these 750 acres are not a hundred miles from civilization.

The park was given by the Rockefeller family estate to the public just a few years ago, and apparently not many people know about it, for it is wonderfully uncrowded. There are some 14 miles of carriage and walking paths, and the beautiful little Swan Lake covers twenty-four acres. There is a variety of terrains, including riverside lanes—the winding Pocantico River makes its way through the park—wetlands, woods, fields, and the path around the lake. Outdoor enthusiasts who use the preserve include birders, photographers, cross-country skiers, and artists, as well as horseback riders.

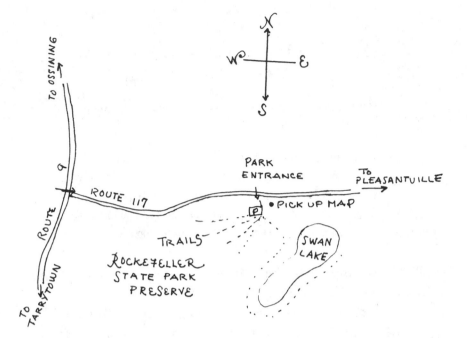

The park asks visitors not to disturb or collect anything. There is no picnicking, but you can take trail lunches to designated areas. Also forbidden are radios, unleashed pets, smoking, motorized vehicles, alcoholic beverages, and camping and swimming. These rules do not seem excessive, for the stillness and cleanliness of the grounds are a wonderful antidote to the bustle of life outside. It is an ideal place for reflection as well as energetic walking. The lakeside, in particular, is an oasis of quiet beauty, where you can watch the expanding ripples of water as a duck swims by.

This is an ideal outing for families, including the elderly and children. Most of the trails (all color marked) are not difficult, and your walk can be as long as you wish to make it, for a good map (available at the entrance in a box on the side of the shed) will allow you to crisscross and combine one trail with another. Take good walking shoes, binoculars, some bread for the ducks if you wish, and perhaps a sketchbook or camera. A number of the trails are listed as steep grades; these provide wonderful upward climbs that will take you to spots from which you will get a panoramic view of the Hudson below. The map at the shed lists the difficulty and length of each trail, so be sure to read it before you set out.

One of the trails will take you along the Old Croton Aqueduct trail (see Outing 18), which runs all the way from Croton to the city. In fact, if you are an adventurous walker—in addition to a strong and energetic one—you can start out at Croton and walk south through woodland and village, through this preserve, and on to 173rd Street in Manhattan. (To take that walk, you should obtain the Old Croton Aqueduct walk directory from New York State Parks, Taconic Region, Staatsburg, NY 12580, or call 914–693–5259.)

We recommend this walk in any season, including winter and in snowy weather. Those folks who enjoy a winter hike can't find a better one than this: parking is easy, the terrain is mostly level, and there are no snowmobiles or other noisy intrusions. Winter birds enjoy the lake and woods. In fall the foliage is glorious, and its reflection in the still lake waters is lovely to look at. Spring and summer are, of course, perfect times to visit, so this is indeed a year-round site for walkers.

The Walk

After leaving your car at the entrance parking area (free), you can choose which trail to take. You'll begin at the parking area. The Swan Lake Trail, a real strolling path, will take you along the edge of the lake and onto Ridge Trail, where you can see the lake from above on a hillside, or onto Ash Tree and Overlook trails. Both are steep paths with panoramic views of the lake. If you start from the parking area on Nature's Way Trail, you'll see some nice rocky areas in a lovely wooded setting. That route can lead you to the old colonial road called Old Sleepy Hollow Trail, a gently sloping roadway. If you continue on that trail and turn left at the fork, you'll come to the Pocantico River, which ripples alongside the path. If you choose the opposite direction, you will find Eagle Hill Trail, a steep climb with a great view of the Hudson as a reward for your efforts.

These are only a few of the twenty different trails identified by the park. We suggest a plan before you start off: Add up the mileage in advance so that you know just how much you can manage and still return in one piece to your car.

After the Walk

This preserve is conveniently close to several tourist attractions. The historic region of Tarrytown (the Sleepy Hollow of earlier times) includes several historic restorations, fine antique homes, Sleepy Hollow Cemetery where Washington Irving is buried, and the wonderful Pocantico Union Church with its Chagall windows. All of these attractions are described in Outing 19. You can visit any of them after your outing, or you might want to combine this walk with the exploration of Sleepy Hollow Cemetery itself (Outing 19).

23 | Unusual Plantings, Waterfalls, and Rocks

Stonecrop Gardens, Cold Spring

How to Get There: From Manhattan take the Henry Hudson Parkway north (it becomes the Saw Mill River Parkway shortly) and follow signs for the Taconic state Parkway. Take the Taconic and exit at Route 301. Go west for about 3 miles. The driveway for Stonecrop is a sharp right, directly opposite Dennytown Road (the sign for Stonecrop is very small and easy to miss).

Anyone who likes gardens should find Stonecrop Gardens inspiring. For rock garden enthusiasts, however, they are a must. A steep hill off a rural road in Putnam County's rolling countryside leads to this enchanting spot. Here, in an unusually idyllic setting, are some of the most glorious alpine and water gardens anywhere.

The Stonecrop estate enjoys pastoral views over meadows to distant hills. The beautifully designed grounds include a French-style country house with adjoining stable and wood fences, an enclosed garden, potting sheds and greenhouses, ponds and a lake, stone walls, plus the gardens. A woodland garden, pond garden, grass garden, and perennial borders are among the many tasteful plantings. But what gives Stonecrop its special cachet are its incredible rock and water gardens and alpine collection.

You'll find a variety of these rock gardens throughout the grounds—from the area next to the house, where the plantings are displayed in tidy beds and in greenhouses, to the magnificent stream and cliff rock gardens beyond. And it's very likely that you won't meet more than a handful of other visitors; you

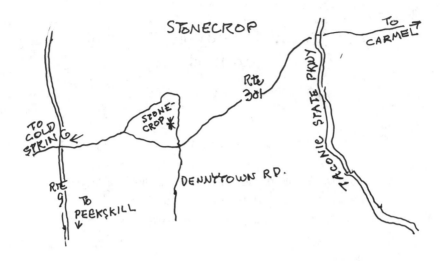

should be able to have the place almost to yourself. For information call (845) 265–2000 or visit www.stonecrop.org.

The Walk

Before embarking on your exploration of Stonecrop, stop at the "office" (located just inside the house) to pay the entrance fee and pick up a map and descriptive guide. You might start with the enclosed garden, accessible from a scenic deck on the side of the house (the panoramic view from here is quite spectacular). Within a high wooden fence is an English-style garden with square and triangular beds containing vegetables and heirloom flowers. You can walk around winding pathways to see espaliers of lindens, dwarf apples and pears, and a romantic grape arbor. Guarding the scene is an effigy of Gertrude Jekyll, the great English landscape designer, made to look curiously like a scarecrow.

A path leads to the greenhouses and raised glass-covered troughs for displaying alpines. The carefully labeled exhibits are of museum quality and include every imaginable variety, most shown in the tiniest of pots in neat rows. If you are interested in learning about these plants in detail or care to embellish your own rock garden, this is a perfect opportunity. (You might even compare notes with one of the gardeners, who can often be found working diligently in this area.)

In front of the house, you'll see other examples of rock gardens. Many are on raised beds supported by stone or limestone (tufa) walls; especially delightful are mini-versions shown on rectangular and round "pedestals."

To reach the most spectacular site of all—the rock ledge and the stream garden that precedes it—walk west from the house. What you see here more dramatically than anywhere else at Stonecrop is the result of an imaginative partnership between nature and human ingenuity. In the 1980s the naturally rocky terrain was enhanced by the addition of yet more rocks, including giant boulders, on the ledge. A network of gently flowing streams and pools was created, emptying into a lake below (with the water recirculating through underground pipes), and thousands of plants—mostly alpines, grasses, dwarf conifers, and Mediterranean species—were carefully placed, for color, texture, and pattern.

The visual effect of the streams gently moving through the delicate plantings, around the rounded rocks, and into the clear pools is magical. But best of all is the fact that you actually walk down the cliff garden, stepping onto rocks that form it; in so doing, you feel more like a participant than a passive observer looking in from the outside. As with the rest of Stonecrop, everything here is beautifully maintained and the plants all labeled, even the tiniest. You can wend your way on a path of stepping stones at water's edge to a charming wood pavilion covered with wisteria and similar in design to the main house (though in a more Japanese vein); this is a good lookout point from which to enjoy the view.

A network of paths continues around the lake, across a rustic stone bridge (known as the "Flintstone" bridge), and down the hillside toward the woodland pond. This lower pond is surrounded by primulas and woodland plants; from it a path leads through a grove of bamboo. You can explore it all at will, consulting your map.

Before leaving Stonecrop, be sure to walk on a small path through the woodland garden: Azaleas, rhododendrons, and other shade-loving plants have been carefully placed to blend harmoniously with this natural habitat. Nearby is a pond surrounded by lilies and groupings of an exotic Brazilian species with giant leaves (apparently the largest herbaceous plant recognized). You would hardly imagine that this delightful pond was once a swamp; it is now maintained by artificial streams at each end. This is yet another example of the care, work, and imagination that have made Stonecrop the rare site it is.

24 | A Chinese Landscape in Dutchess County

Innisfree Garden, Millbrook

How to Get There: From midtown Manhattan, take the Henry Hudson Parkway north (it becomes the Saw Mill River Parkway shortly) and follow signs for the Taconic State Parkway. Take the Taconic exit at Poughkeepsie/Millbrook (Route 44), and go east on Route 44. Look for Tyrrel Road on your right. The entrance to Innisfree is from Tyrrel Road.

The artistic gardens of Innisfree, near Millbrook, are well worth a foray into the countryside. Created in the 1920s to reflect the philosophy and aesthetic of Chinese gardens, they bring you to a very different world than that of most gardens in our region. Experiencing Innisfree means taking an inspiring journey and exploring nature through ancient Chinese artistic tradition. In fact, a walk here is akin to finding a series of Chinese landscape paintings that are real and three-dimensional, and then strolling right into them.

Walter Beck, a painter, and his wife, Marion, spent twenty-five years creating these vast gardens. Their inspiration came primarily from the eighth-century Chinese scrolls of the poet/painter Wang Wei, where scenes in nature are unfolded gradually. The basic design idea of Innisfree is the "cup garden"—a Chinese tradition dating back hundreds of years. The Chinese would set apart an object by "framing" it in such a way that it would be distinct and apart from its surroundings. According to Lester Collins, the landscape architect who has been in charge of Innisfree for many years, "You build a picture

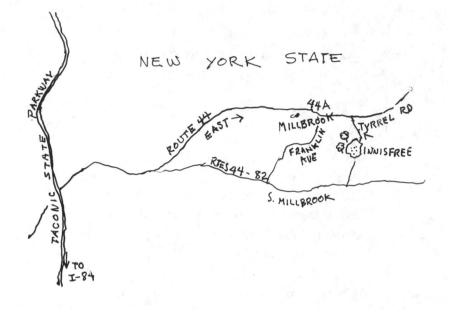

of nature; you control the floor and the walls, and you bring the sky down."

Walking through Innisfree is analogous to walking through an art gallery from one picture to the next—from a meadow to a rock covered with moss, to a lotus pool—in each case concentrating on the element before you. As with a work of art, each destination has been carefully created to affect the viewer's senses in a certain way. Nature has been tamed completely, and even though the terrain at Innisfree may look wild and free, nothing has been left to chance. The land has been cleared, and waterfalls, streams, and pools have been created. "In their gardens," says Collins, "the Chinese express life and death and everything together—the pain and the wonder." The two main elements of Chinese gardens, mountains and rocks (yang) and water (yin), are very important in this garden and provide the necessary counterpoint of life. Yin is passive, dark, and moist; yang is active, bright, and aggressive. According to the Chinese, a harmonious arrangement of mountains and water can give the viewer a spiritual experience of universal harmony. Water and rocks of all sizes and shapes are everywhere, set amid soft foliage, shrubs, and trees. Flowers are not an important element in Chinese gardens, but here you will find delicate clematis growing on an arbor, primroses, water irises, forget-me-nots, and hydrangeas.

Innisfree is a garden for all seasons, since it emphasizes the architecture of its basic elements in harmony with one another. (Note, however, that it is only open May through October.) You can enjoy it under any weather conditions, as a great garden "is good aesthetically and has nothing to do with climate," according to Collins. In fact, on one of our visits we experienced torrential rains. But the downpours only echoed the usual sounds of the nearby streams and waterfalls, and the soft colors of the foliage were rendered the more vivid by the rain. For information call (845) 677–8000 or visit www.innisfreegarden.com.

The Walk

Before setting out on your walk, you can pick up a map near the parking lot. A network of paths will take you around the lake (from where you'll see a tantalizing little island of pines that can be explored) and up and down gently sloping hills. Chinese gardens are supposed to be miniatures of nature's way; here, too, you will walk past small evocations of mountains, streams, and forests, experiencing each sensation as a traveler might in the open countryside, or as a viewer who encounters an unfolding Chinese handscroll landscape painting. You'll come across a mist fountain, a rock garden waterfall, a curious "Fu Dog" stone statue, a hillside cave, a brick terrace (where you can rest and take in the view), fantastic rocks in the shapes of turtles and dragons, bird and bat houses, water sculptures, and hemlock woods. Don't fail to look about you at distant views as well.

The Hudson Valley (West)

25 | An Autumn Outing in the Footsteps of the Hudson River Artists

Kaaterskill Falls

How to Get There: From the George Washington Bridge, take the Palisades Interstate Parkway to the New York State Thruway north and exit at Saugerties (exit 20). Take Route 32 north to Palenville, and Route 23A west toward Haines Falls. After about 3.5 miles, you'll see a small sign on the right-hand side of the road indicating the way to Kaaterskill Falls (you will also see a gorge and another waterfall). Go another 0.25 mile until you reach a parking area on the left side of the road. Walk down to the sign indicating the falls.

When American painters celebrated the glories of our land-scape more than a century ago, it was the Hudson River Valley and the Catskill Mountain region that inspired them. The rushing waterfalls, jagged rocks and cliffs, and beautiful trees of the region became the subject for dozens of paintings, many of them as beloved (or more) today as when they first appeared.

Happily, that landscape still exists, much of it unspoiled and protected; in fact, some areas have an entirely new growth of for-est. The Hudson River artists would be elated (as we were) to dis-cover the same breathtaking lookouts and rugged forest paths.

We decided to follow the footsteps of a number of them in the Kaaterskill Falls region that they immortalized. Our walk was probably more difficult than theirs (notwithstanding paint box, sketchbook, and easel in tow), since conservation efforts have closed some trails, and the train and convenient horse and buggy routes have been discontinued. In the nineteenth century, during the heyday of the grand Catskill hotels, guests would arrive by train, get off near the head of the falls, and walk down a short distance to view them. However, we persevered on foot, and it was well worth it!

There are three particularly spectacular parts of the Kaaterskill walk. One, of course, is the falls, a magical hidden spot that looks quite the same as when painted by Thomas Cole, the "father" of the Hudson River school. The falls, with the two-part cascade over the rosy stone mountainside, were painted three times by Cole, as well as by other artists, making them one of the most famous nineteenth-century landscape subjects of all. If before or after your visit you would like to see how Kaaterskill Falls looked to the artists, there are several books on the Hudson River school with fine reproductions, such as Cole's drawings of them (now at the Detroit Institute of Arts) and three paintings (one of which is in Tuscaloosa, Alabama, at the Warner Collection). You'll also find a painting by Sanford Gifford, a Hudson River artist of the next generation, at the Metropolitan Museum. Later, Winslow Homer and Currier & Ives created their own versions of the falls.

Many of the artists stayed at the most famous hotel of the period, the Mountain House, a columned and elegant hostelry set literally on the edge of one of the great cliffs and overlooks of the Hudson Valley, another dramatic spot. We climbed to the very site of the inn (no longer there, alas) and stared out at the ribbon of the Hudson in the distance and the spectacular scenery below us. Our third scenic location is reached by taking the trail (see below for details) from the site of the hotel along the cliff toward a wonderful rocky plateau appropriately called Artist Rock. We could imagine the artists' excitement at a vista almost too beautiful to paint. Along the way to Artist Rock we passed several sites, quite overgrown now, from which they could see the great hotel in the distance. Jasper Cropsey painted it (Minneapolis Museum of Art), Cole drew it (Brooklyn Museum),

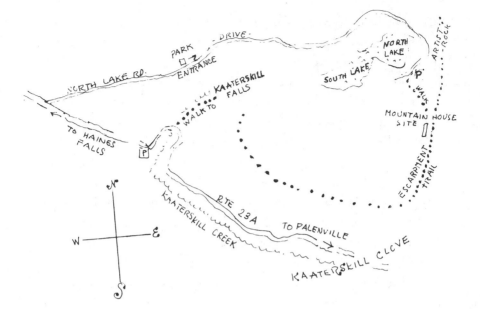

and Sanford Gifford painted it in autumn glory (Trinity College, Hartford). Unfortunately, the hotel's rates became too steep for the artists, many of whom bought homes in the area instead and continued to paint the region around it anyway.

The entire scenic region lies along Kaaterskill Creek, which makes its way between rolling mountains quite close to the Hudson. As you drive there you'll take a winding mountain road (known as Rip Van Winkle Trail) through another oft-painted spot, Kaaterskill Clove. (*Clove,* widely used in this Dutch-settled region, is a ravine or mountain gully, after the Dutch for *cleft.*) Kaaterskill Clove (pictured by Asher Durand in probably the most famous Hudson Valley painting of all, *Kindred Spirits*) is a scenic convergence of glorious trees, craggy mountains, gorges, a narrow serpentine river, and jutting rocks. Kaaterskill Clove was painted so often that there must have been artists at every turn! Among the most famous works are another one by Durand called *Kaaterskill Clove* (belonging to the private Century Association of New York City); Cole's *The Clove, Catskills* (at the New Britain Museum of Art, New Britain, Connecticut); and *Kauterskill Clove,* by Sanford Gifford (at the Metropolitan Museum in New York).

You will enjoy searching out these and other works and tracking their locations in this area. Some of the sites are now unreachable; for example, about a quarter mile of the Escarpment Trail that the artists and others once took from the Mountain House across the mountain to the top of the falls is no longer open to walkers, who now must climb up from the bottom. However, the exact spot where each artist set up to view the clove, or the many unspecific views of woods and mountains (which we know were made in the neighborhood), would be a fine research project for a hardy walker, reproductions in hand.

We settled for the three most famous locales and were well rewarded for our hikes through some rough terrain. The description below will give you an idea of how to go about tracking the artists of our past.

This three-part walk, being one of our more rugged ventures, is recommended for those who are in relatively good physical condition. Be sure to wear sturdy shoes and bring drinking water along! The best time to go is during the fall, at the peak of foliage. Summers tend to be crowded with campers and hikers; the snowy and icy paths become too arduous in winter; and the going is too wet in spring. Try to go on a weekday, if possible, as weekends are busy with walkers in summer and fall.

The Walk

For the first part, park your car at the public parking area on Route 23A, about 3.5 miles after leaving Palenville and Route 32. Walk downhill about 0.25 mile to a small bridge overlooking Kaaterskill Creek and Bastion Falls, which are quite grand in themselves. You will see a smallish sign indicating Kaaterskill

Falls to be 0.5 mile up from there (it seemed longer to us). On the other side of the road is a wonderful view of Kaaterskill Clove, perhaps one of the same views admired and painted by the Hudson River artists.

Walk uphill, following the rather sporadic yellow trail markers, which lead you more or less parallel to the creek all the way to the falls. (If you lose sight of the trail markers, which is likely, keep walking next to the creek and you won't get lost.) The going is quite arduous, as the "path" (which is hardly one at all) has been eroded and footing is uneven. You clamber over large rocks, twisted tree roots, decaying branches, and leaves, which can be slippery. Even though the distance is fairly short, the trek will be difficult for those who are not in fairly good physical condition. (We saw some poor souls trying to negotiate their climb on all fours!) But your efforts are well rewarded. The forest is dense with hemlocks and many deciduous trees that illuminate it with bright colors in the fall. As you make the rugged but exhilarating climb up, you feel somewhat like an explorer in a primeval forest.

Finally, you reach a large boulder in the middle of the creek bed from where you get a full front view of the falls in all their splendor. And what majestic falls they are! At 260 feet, they are the highest in New York State (including Niagara Falls, which, however, are much broader, of course). The two slender and elegant cascades are divided by a rock basin and surrounded by a landscape that is wild, rugged, and uncorrupted—truly a quintessential romantic scene. After you have stopped long enough to rest and take in this marvelous site, you must retrace your steps, since you can no longer proceed up alongside the falls for a side view.

As we descended the hill, we felt elated and ready to see more. If you feel the same way, drive up to the North Lake State Campsite, a park from which you can walk to the site where the

Mountain House once stood, only a few miles away. To reach the park from Route 23A, continue in the same direction to Haines Falls and take a right on Route 18, following signs for the North Lake State Campsite. You arrive at an efficient-looking tollbooth where you pay a small fee and are given a map and trail guide that shows you (more or less) how to find the Mountain House site. You have now entered Catskill State Park, a woodsy region popular with campers and hikers and filled with clearly marked trails. Park at North Lake, where the road comes to an end. You'll see a small sandy beach, picnic and restroom facilities, and signs telling you what is prohibited (just about everything except hiking). To reach the Mountain House site, follow the signs up a gentle hill until you come to the commemorative marker for the hotel. Continue toward the escarpment for what has been—and continues to be—regarded as one of the most impressive and vast panoramas in the East. The landscape seems to go on forever: Miles of the glistening Hudson are laid out in front of you, surrounded by the lush river valley. Beyond you can see the Taconic and Berkshire ranges.

After gazing at this remarkable view for some time, we ventured forth, map in hand, toward Artist Rock (about 0.5 mile away, on the Escarpment Trail) to see if we could find a good view of the Catskill Mountain House site. Follow the signs for Artist Rock, Sunset Rock, and Newmans Ledge, trails all quite clearly marked with blue blazes. Once you are past picnic areas and other indications of organized parkland, you find yourself on virgin, somewhat hilly terrain along the cliffs, from where you have one extraordinary view after another, including several from which the Mountain House site could have been seen. After a short but arduous climb on top of large boulders (but, fortunately, not near the edge of the cliff!), you reach a plateau which appears almost to be (but isn't) a man-made terrace, so regular is the rock surface. Continue until you come to what is unmistakably Artist Rock, another great lookout point over a ledge. The trees around it are now overgrown, making it difficult to see the Mountain House site, but you can imagine that this may have been a particularly dramatic vista some hundred years ago. If you wish, continue on to Sunset Rock and Newmans Ledge.

If you are still able and adventuresome, go back to the hotel site and set out on the other section of the Escarpment Trail. It used to be possible to reach the falls from above, along a network of trails that still exist. This extensive trail system includes miles of fabulous views atop tall cliffs overlooking the Hudson River Valley and Kaaterskill Clove. The hike from the Catskill Mountain House site to the falls is about 4 miles, but the trail along the ledges is difficult and dangerous, and the section of it that actually goes to the falls was recently definitively closed as unsafe, so your walk will not reach the falls from above. Still, you will not be disappointed, for the part you can still do is spectacular.

After the Walk

While in a Hudson River artist's frame of mind, you might want to take a detour and visit Olana, the home of Frederick Church, one of the more flamboyant (and also more successful) exponents of that school. Built in 1874, this eclectic and eccentric house is a sort of Moorish Victorian creation filled to the brim with furnishings and bric-a-brac that Church collected in his world travels. Aside from its more "kitschy" aspects, it does house some very fine paintings by Church and other Hudson River artists and is an amusing place to visit. The view from the house (perched 500 feet above the Hudson) and its 250-acre park is special.

The park is open to the public for boating, picnicking, and nature walks; the house is open April through October, Tuesday through Sunday 10:00 A.M. to 5:00 P.M., by tour only; phone:

(518) 828–0135. Olana is about 5 miles south of the city of Hudson on the east side of the Hudson River. To get there from Kaaterskill Falls, retrace your route and get back on the New York State Thruway, go north, and exit at Catskill (exit 21), where you can cross the river. Take Route 9G north for a few miles and follow the signs.

26 | An Off-Season Lake Walk

Rockland Lake, Congers

How to Get There: Take the George Washington Bridge to the Palisades Interstate Parkway, exit 4. Go north on Route 9W about 9 miles. Access to Rockland State Park is off Route 9W and is well marked, and there are several parking areas.

The Rockland Lake walk is a pleasant circular 3-mile jaunt along the edge of the water. The lake lies within Rockland Lake State Park, 588 acres of somewhat developed parklands with sports and picnic facilities. During busy summer weekends the park is crowded and noisy with the sounds of blaring radios. For this reason we recommend this outing off-season or on week-days, when it is wonderfully peaceful. This is a flat, easy walk that will appeal to joggers, bikers, and nature lovers.

Rockland Lake is a post-glacial lake, once famous for the excellent quality of the ice produced here in the days before refrigeration. In fact, its ice was exported not only to nearby areas, but also as far away as the Caribbean. The remnants of icehouses used to store the ice can still be seen in the park.

Although you are never really far from "civilization," this lakeside walk is still bucolic. Willows line the path, and there are peaceful views of fishermen in rowboats, surrounded by water lilies. There are ducks, swans, and geese everywhere, encour-aged by families with children who bring food for them. In the fall you might see mute swans, originally domesticated birds from Europe, that live in pairs and sometimes reach the age of one hundred.

Avoid the weekends of July and August! Otherwise, this is an all-season outing. If you plan to do more than walk—you can

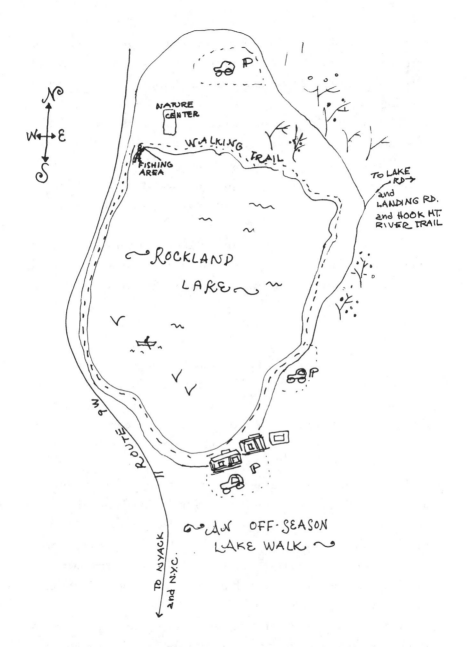

N

W E

S

P

NATURE CENTER

WALKING TRAIL

FISHING AREA

TO LAKE RD.

and LANDING RD. and HOOK MT. RIVER TRAIL

~ROCKLAND

LAKE ~

P

ROUTE 9W

P

~AN OFF·SEASON LAKE WALK ~

TO NYACK and N.Y.C.

fish, ice-skate, row a boat, or watch for birds—you should check
to see when those activities are available. (Call 845–268–3020
for general information.) Birders should go between March

and October; there is ice-fishing on cold winter days; and you can rent a rowboat, rain or shine, from April to the end of October. Winter is especially nice if there's not a cold wind blowing.

This is an outing for people of any age or physical ability. The less energetic will enjoy ambling along this mostly shaded path at a leisurely pace; children will like feeding the waterfowl; nature lovers can look for various species of flora and fauna. Others might just like to be in a quiet setting with pleasant views at every turn.

If you are a birder, bring binoculars. Bring along a picnic; there are several lakeside picnic tables, but you will also find plenty of shade trees to sit under or lookout points from which to enjoy the view.

The Walk

Park either near the swimming pool and bathhouse or by the fishing and comfort station. You can't miss the path: In addition to being a footpath, it is a bike trail and marked as such. It doesn't matter in which direction you start, or at what point you begin your walk, as you will eventually come back to your starting point.

Take in your surroundings: the many wonderful wildflowers and shrubs that bloom along the path during June, the trees reflected in the lake, and the sounds of birds overhead. You might be able to identify some of the following species: downy woodpecker, song sparrow, red-winged blackbird, tree swallow, mockingbird, yellow warbler, Baltimore oriole, goldfinch, catbird, and swamp sparrow.

Eventually you will come to the nature center, a smallish wooden structure at the north side of the lake. There you can see displays of live snakes, toads, frogs, fish, and salamanders indigenous to these parts. From the nature center there are two marshy trails (totaling about a half mile) that take you through a woodland swamp. You walk atop a boardwalk through dark woods, past a variety of plants that are identified on markers. You'll see spicebush (early settlers made tea from its fragrant twigs and leaves), red maples, white ash, red oaks, tulip trees, swamp loosestrife, ferns, and red osiers.

It is a pleasant surprise to come upon a clearing and good view of the lake, from where the second trail begins. This lakeside bog trail, a shaded leafy walk with a canopy of shrubs overhead, takes you past wild flowering bushes, swamp azaleas, arrowwood (used by Indians for arrow shafts), high-bush blueberry, and winterberry. There is a lovely second lookout point where you might want to pause briefly to enjoy the scenery. The path leads back to the main lakeside walk, where you can continue, if you like.

After the Walk

You might want to take advantage of the other activities Rockland Lake can provide. There is excellent fishing in both winter and summer. Licenses, available at local sporting goods stores, are required. Since 1980 the lake has been stocked with hybrid muskellunge, chain pickerel, bass, perch, and sunfish. You can rent a rowboat and tackle from April through October, seven days a week, regardless of the weather.

27 | Strolling through a Sculpturescape

Storm King Art Center, Mountainville

How to Get There: From the George Washington Bridge, take the Palisades Interstate Parkway north to the New York State Thruway. Take exit 16 (Harriman) to Route 32 north and go about 10 miles. Follow the signs to Storm King Art Center (first left after a small bridge, onto Orrs Mill Road, then another left onto Old Pleasant Hill Road).

You're driving on winding roads through the rolling country-side in the Hudson Valley. Suddenly you find yourself in front of an extraordinary place where large, brilliant, imposing struc-tures reach up to the sky in a startling contrast to the environ-ment. You are at the Storm King Art Center, probably the most impressive and important outdoor sculpture park and museum in the United States.

It would be hard to imagine a place where works of art are more dramatically displayed. Located 55 miles north of New York City in a valley between Storm King and Schunemunk mountains, the center encompasses a collection of more than 200 modern sculptures, many of massive proportions. They are set in an expansive landscape of grassy hills and vast fields, sur-rounded by acres of woodland. Walking through the spacious grounds (some 400 acres) and seeing these giant abstract sculp-tures perched atop hills and spread out in valleys below is an inspiring, if startling, visual experience. Mostly made of metal and stone in massive geometric forms, these sculptures tower like stark visitors from another world. We can think of no real equivalent to Storm King Art Center. While there are other sculpture gardens in America and Europe, most are smaller in

scale and more urban in setting. There is something quintessentially American about the combination of space and contemporary art.

The center, founded in 1960, occupies the grounds of what
was formerly the residence of one Vermont Hatch. His elegant
Normandy-style chateau, built in 1935 with the stones from a
nearby Hudson River mansion destined for demolition, is now
used to display traveling sculpture exhibitions, as well as some of
the more delicate pieces of the permanent collection. Hatch's
great friend and neighbor, Ted Ogden (a businessman, farmer,
world traveler, and art collector), gradually converted this wonderful estate into a sculpture museum, after having been
inspired by photographs showing Henry Moore sculptures on a
sheep ranch in Scotland. In a major coup, he acquired fourteen
pieces of sculpture by the late David Smith at one time, gener-
ating a great deal of interest for the museum. To this group he
added important works by such contemporary sculptors as
Alexander Calder, Anthony Caro, Mark di Suvero, Charles
Ginnever, Robert Grosvenor, Barbara Hepworth, Henry
Moore, David Von Schlegell, and Isaac Witkin, to name a few.
Since Ogden's death in 1974, more sculptures have found their
permanent home at Storm King. As they are added, more land
is cleared, hills are created or altered to accommodate them,
and new paths are built. The landscape of Storm King is ever-
changing.

One of the wonderful things here is that you can go right up to
the sculptures—if you have the stamina to cover the necessary distances—or you can view them from afar. You can take a one-hour
guided walking tour for a fee, Wednesday through Sunday from
May 1 to mid-November. (Reservations are required; call
845–534–3190.) However, we think that it's more fun to roam
on your own throughout this vast place and to see whatever appeals
to you. You can wander for miles up and down the various hills, or

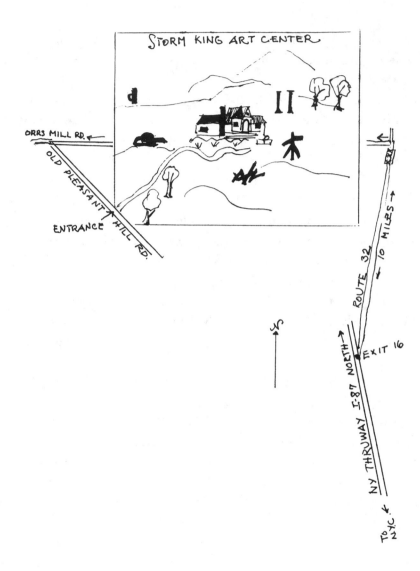

you can limit yourself to the particular areas that interest you. (At the entrance you'll find a map that shows you where to find what.)

This walk can be as leisurely or as arduous as you make it, depending on what you want to cover. It's an excursion that most people would enjoy; of course, art lovers will find it most stimulating, but so will many others—particularly foreign visitors—

who will be intrigued by this unique environment. Children will find it great fun to traipse up and down hills, past structures like none they may have ever seen before. Though there are some signs requesting specifically that you not touch a particular work, others have no such restrictions. In fact, an impressive work by Isamu Noguchi, *Momo Taro,* has been partially hollowed out so that the visitor can actually sit inside it!

When you go to Storm King you should take a picnic, as there are tables in grassy areas near the lower parking lot (and few restaurants in the vicinity). The center is open daily, except Tuesdays, from April 1 to November 30, from noon to 5:30 P.M. (In winter, when the museum is closed, the smaller, more delicate sculptures are taken inside; others are wrapped up like suburban shrubbery; and the hardier are left outside as they are, to brave the elements.) Because of the spaciousness of the grounds, you never have the impression of crowds outside. Of course, the inside museum—with its limited space—is likely to be busy on weekends.

For more information, call (845) 534–3115.

The Walk

After parking your car, proceed to the main house, which is Storm King's entrance and center. There you pay a small fee and pick up whatever literature you wish, including a guide to the museum. Start off in the immediate vicinity of the house, where the smaller, more intimate sculptures are displayed. Close to the entrance is a fine piece by Louise Nevelson, which you should not miss, as well as some more representational works by such artists as Emilio Greco, Jo Davidson, and Henri Etienne-Martin, placed around the house amid formal gardens. Nearby you will see a group of Ionic columns, which look like sculptures themselves. We were told they come from the original estate that provided some of the building material for the house. The columns look perfect in this setting, adding a touch of romanticism to the scene. On the other side of the house you'll find a group of David Smith sculptures, which invariably attract the largest number of visitors. (Only eight of the Smith sculptures are displayed outside; the others, which are more delicate, can be seen indoors.)

As you go beyond the more formal garden space next to the house, the landscape becomes freer and more open, as well as more hilly. An intermediate (in size) group of works by such sculptors as Henry Moore and Alexander Calder are within the middle distance from the house. As you go farther from the house, the works become larger and more commanding. Noguchi's *Momo Taro* is dramatically placed on a knoll overlooking a valley. The massive pieces by Alexander Liberman (*Ascent, Eve,* and *Adonai*) are on the outer edges of the cleared grounds; Tal Streeter's bright orange *Endless Column* zigzags its way up to the sky, towering over trees; Mark di Suvero's gigantic works are in a distant valley below the house, and a walk to view them up close is quite a trek.

Walking through this incredible landscape stimulates thought on the nature of art and the function of art in nature. Are these works in harmony with their natural environment, or are they an imposition on it? Does the place work as a setting for such art? No matter what conclusions you draw, we are sure that you will not be disappointed in your outing at Storm King.

After the Walk

You might want to take a look at West Point Military Academy, since it's so close. To get to West Point, follow scenic Route 218 through the village of Cornwall, going south for a few miles. Roads are clearly marked. Stop at the visitor center at the entrance and pick up a map for a self-guided walking or driving tour. We suggest you drive around the sprawling campus—which resembles a fortified castle, with crenellated towers—before you park, to get oriented. There are lovely views of the Hudson at every turn. Points of interest include Academy Chapel, with its Gothic-style features, brick and stone interior arches, high vaulted ceilings, and stained-glass windows; the Thayer Museum, across campus; and Trophy Point, overlooking the river, where links of iron chains were used to prevent British ships from coming up the river during the Revolutionary War. (See Outing 29 for the origin of the iron.) But the most fun is to view the marching cadets in their familiar uniforms. If you go on a weekend, especially in fall (when there might be a football game), be prepared for the inevitable crowds. West Point is open daily from 9:00 A.M. to 4:30 P.M., and there is no admission charge.

28 | Along a Railroad Track
by the Hudson
Piermont

How to Get There: Take the George Washington Bridge, to the Palisades Interstate Parkway. Get off at exit 4, and go north on Route 9W. After about 3.3 miles (you will pass a bridge and two sets of traffic lights) there is a sharp right-hand turn off of Route 9W (Ash Street in Piermont). The sign reads PEIRMONT BUSINESS DISTRICT. Go down a steep hill to the center of the village.

You may remember walking along a railroad track as a child, including the frightening moment when you walked across the wooden trestle. An abandoned track through rural countryside evokes a bygone era of America.

In Piermont, only 17 miles from New York City, you can amble along a former railroad track bed—called the Erie Path—high above the Hudson, overlooking the Victorian frame houses that line the river. Coming back, we suggest you go down to River Road and enjoy the river and the houses up close. This walk is mostly flat, except for where you descend to river level and return to railroad track level to pick up your car. What is surprising is how solitary this path is, except for an occasional jogger or bird-watcher. The tracks here were originally built by the Erie Railroad, the first long-distance railroad in the United States, connecting two ports: Piermont (as its easternmost point) and Dunkirk, New York, on the shores of Lake Erie, some 450 miles to the west. The railroad was formally inaugurated in Piermont on May 14, 1851, amid great pomp with many illustrious guests, including President Millard Fillmore and his secretary of state, Daniel Webster. Thousands of people lined

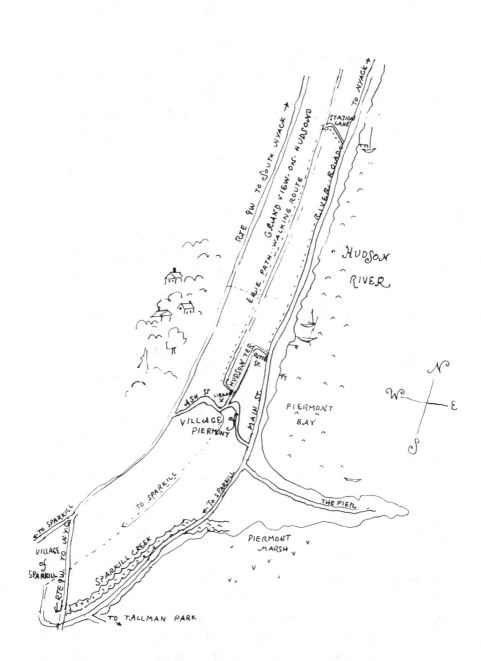

the streets to catch a glimpse of the event. Several dignitaries then took the train to Dunkirk, where another huge celebration around a 300-foot dining table awaited them.

Piermont and the other towns along the route all prospered as a result of the railroad, but these boom years were short. By 1861 the railroad's major commercial traffic went to New Jersey destinations rather than to the Hudson Valley, and this section of the line was used for commuter traffic only (by then many city dwellers had already become exurbanites). This commuter rail line, called the North Branch, operated from Nyack to Jersey City until the 1960s, when it was abandoned. In 1975 it was designated a park and has been enjoyed by walkers, joggers, and even occasional horseback riders ever since.

This is a leafy, shady walk in spring and fall, and a sparkling, dramatic walk in winter. It's often very hot and humid in summer. It is not an arduous hike and is mostly flat, but it does include some hills. The distance varies, depending on where you leave your car. At its shortest and flattest it's a 2-mile round-trip (if you don't go down to the river). We recommend this walk for fairly energetic people who appreciate nature, views, and looking at Victorian houses.

This outing requires good walking shoes, insect repellent (in summer), and water. While you can picnic along the wooded trail, there are no places to stop for a picnic along River Road; this is an area of private homes. Piermont offers several pleasant eating places.

The Walk

You have two options, depending on how energetic you feel and how much time you have:

For a 5 mile round-trip, drive back to Sparkill (south) via Piermont's River Road (Piermont Avenue) alongside the creek. When you reach the railroad tracks in Sparkill, park your car near the crossing. You'll find a small dirt path, which marks the beginning of the Erie Path. As you walk through this pleasant woodland way above the villages of Sparkill and Piermont, notice the wide variety of trees around you: tulip, beech, oak, ash, birch, mulberry, locust, and dogwood.

Although heavily wooded, the trail has occasional clearings with expanses of wild honeysuckle, mock orange, wild roses, smart weed, dayflowers, wild grapevines, and raspberries. You'll find birds, rabbits, and other small creatures along this path as well.

After about 1 mile you'll come to a brief interruption in the trail, where a paved road (Ash Street) cuts across, but continue straight ahead on the Erie Path past the old station (now a private house). After another mile or so you'll reach a trestle, which overlooks a dramatic ravine, where you might like to stop and take in the view. This is especially scenic in winter, when you have excellent visibility of the gorge. After about 0.5 mile you'll come to two fences across the road, which you can go around easily. Look for a small path to the right just beyond. This is Station Lane (unmarked as such), which cuts rather precipitously down the hill and eventually connects with River Road along the Hudson. Station Lane is for those who are sure of foot. Watch for poison ivy!

When you reach River Road, turn right and proceed south, along this charming winding street past the Victorian houses. You will come to the center of the village of Piermont after about 1.5 miles. Find your way back to your car, following the road along Sparkill Creek.

If you decide that a 5 mile walk is too much, try a shorter version of not more than 3.5 miles. We suggest you park near the Piermont library (off Ash Street) and walk to your left until you see the old train station. You will find the Erie Path next to it. For an even shorter walk, do just a portion of the Erie Path and simply retrace your steps. You can always drive past the old houses on River Road.

After the Walk

Tallman Mountain State Park, contiguous to Piermont, can be reached by foot from a dirt road next to the Piermont marsh or by car from Rockland Road right off Route 9W. It is well worth a detour. There are playing fields for various sports; a large swimming pool (next to the river); tennis courts; scenic trails for jogging, cross-country skiing, and biking (follow green signs for the bike route); and picnic grounds overlooking the Hudson.

The historic town of Tappan, a couple of miles south and west of Piermont, is an authentic and unspoiled village originally settled by the Dutch in the seventeenth century. Here you can walk through the historic district in a relatively short time and visit some of the old houses and monuments.

Start with the DeWint House (where you can pick up a hand-out describing the various historic sites). Built in 1700, this is the oldest house in Rockland County.

George Washington used it as his army headquarters on several occasions during the Revolutionary War, and it was here that he condemned Major John Andre to death for being a spy. The old stone-and-brick cottage with green shutters is surrounded by pleasantly shaded grounds, old-fashioned flower gardens, and tall stately trees (copper beech, Norway spruces, magnolias, locusts, white pines, Chinese elms, maples, and Canadian hemlocks). An immense weeping willow, said to be the largest of its kind in the country, stands next to the carriage house. For information call (845) 359–1359.

Near the DeWint House you'll find the Tappan library, dating from 1750, with its authentic colonial garden. Just down the road you'll come to the Yoast Mabie Tavern, known as the '76 House (now a restaurant), where Major Andre was imprisoned.

On the village green you'll see the Reformed Church of Tappan, originally built in the late seventeenth century and then rebuilt in the nineteenth. Next to it are the old burying grounds, where you can wander around past old grave sites. Opposite the green stands the Manse, built in 1724 and in continuous use since then.

29 | Hiking on an Old Iron Mine Trail in the Ramapo Hills

Harriman State Park

How to Get There: From the George Washington Bridge, take the Palisades Interstate Parkway north. Follow the signs for Route 6 west (exit 18). Almost immediately you will come to a traffic circle. Go around most of the circle and take Seven Lakes Drive. After about 4 miles you will come to two lakes on either side of the road. The parking area you want is to your right, next to Lake Skannatati.

This 3 mile circular hike combines an interesting bit of history with a beautiful natural setting. Harriman State Park in the Ramapo Hills is filled with historic sites, among them a great many nineteenth-century iron mines. In this region iron mining, which began in the mid-eighteenth century, had become an important industry by the time of the Revolutionary War, when about 14 percent of the entire world's supply of iron ore was produced here. The area was not only endowed with massive supplies of the mineral, but also the plentiful waterways for powering furnaces and large forests for making the needed charcoal made it a perfect place for iron production. Some of its present-day scenic and recreational lakes were once ponds and streams that were dammed for water supplies.

By the mid-nineteenth century, mines and blast furnaces proliferated, including the Arden Furnace, now called Clove Iron Furnace (see below). For those who worked in the mines (mostly Irish immigrants, including boys as young as eleven), conditions were harsh at best. The work was arduous, winters rugged, and disease rampant. Many died of malaria or black fly

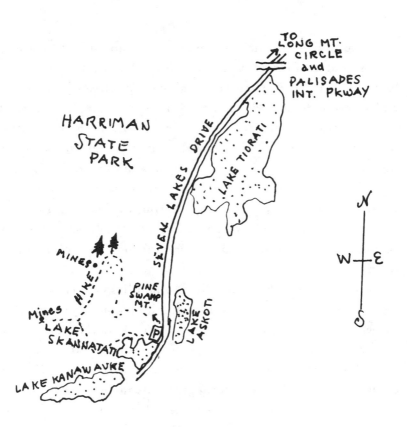

disease spread by mosquitoes from nearby swamps. And the land was ravaged: Masses of trees were cut down, and mines were blasted continually. It's hard to imagine that what is now a truly peaceful stretch of forests and lakes was, only a hundred years ago, a smoldering and denuded wasteland.

The mines in the region were abandoned in the late 1880s, when iron mining proved more profitable and efficient near the anthracite coal beds of Pennsylvania. The Harriman family bought many thousands of acres in the Ramapo region at auction, and gradually—from the early 1900s on—gave up large parcels to be used for public parkland.

Today, 80-square-mile Harriman State Park provides the walker, hiker, and naturalist with a wonderful variety of trails in a vast, unusually scenic environment of mountains, streams, forests, and (man-made) pristine lakes. Because the terrain is hilly with some fairly strenuous climbing and uneven footing, the walk is recommended for those who are used to rougher hikes.

The excursion we recommend includes only a few of the numerous iron mines, but enough to give you an idea of what they were like. They vary in depth from a few feet to hundreds, even thousands, of feet. Some are like caves that you can actually enter; others are simply holes in the ground. That so many have survived erosion is probably due to the fact that wood beams and retaining walls were often built around them to prevent their caving in.

This hike is one that will appeal to families with children, as well as to fit walkers. Children will love the adventuresome aspect of discovering the mines as they go along. However, they should be cautioned to be careful, as many of the mines are not sealed. It might be fun to take along a magnet to test rocks next to the mines for iron ore content. (This method, in fact, was one of several used to determine where to locate mines. Another was to look for rocks that appeared rusty.)

If you are interested, you might also want to take a plumb line, to test the depth of the mines you pass along the way. In addition, we suggest you use a trail map of Harriman State Park, even though the trails are clearly marked. (You can get one either by mail from the New York–New Jersey Trail Conference, P.O. Box 2250, New York, NY 10116, or by visiting the central office at Bear Mountain State Park, next to Harriman.) There are wonderful spots for picnics atop large boulders, or in shaded glades of evergreens, or overlooking a lake. Wear hiking clothes, especially sturdy hiking boots.

This is an outing for all seasons and all days of the week. The area is vast, so you are never overwhelmed by crowds, even at busy times of the year. We especially enjoyed this hike in fall, because of the incredible colors of nature, and in winter, when the tracks of deer and other animals could be seen in the pristine snow.

The Walk

Leave your car at the parking area for boating and fishing next to Lake Skannatati (Lake Askoti is across the road). There are two trails that begin at the northern corner of the parking area. Take the Arden-Surebridge Trail, marked by a white blaze with red dots. You will begin a somewhat strenuous climb up Pine Swamp Mountain; at the summit are some spectacular glacial boulders. You will come to a lovely lookout point to view serene Lake Skannatati below. Continue on the path, which meanders up and down hills, through forests, and past streams for a little more than a mile. You will reach what used to be a logging road for transporting wood from the forest. Go left on this flat, somewhat wide swath, still the Arden-Surebridge Trail. Begin now to look for iron mines. The ones along the trail—which are actually fairly small—look like large holes, averaging maybe 10 feet in diameter, surrounded by rocks and trees. In fact, some hikers might not realize what they are and walk right past them.

Cross a stream and bear left onto a new trail, the Dunning Trail, marked by yellow blazes. This section of the walk is much easier, as you continue along the logging road for a bit. To your left you see the peaceful-looking Pine Swamp, which was a breeding ground for the mosquito plagues the miners had to endure. If you are willing to abandon the trail momentarily in order to locate one of the more spectacular cavelike mines, go up the slope on your right (actually an old tailing pile), until you come to a rocky cliff surrounded by a large mine hole, now filled with water and debris, and a dramatic cave to the left. If you look inside the hillside cave (to which the more intrepid might wish to climb), you will see on your left drill marks from mining days.

After exploring this site, return to the yellow-flagged trail, which continues on along the swamp. Soon you will come to a fork. If you were to continue on Dunning (yellow) Trail, which is certainly worthwhile but commits you to a much longer hike, you would bear to the right. For our shorter hike we suggest you bear left onto a blue-blaze route, which is part of the Long Path. The trail is somewhat rocky and goes up and down, but is not difficult. You pass through varied scenery of open areas, mountain laurel, forests, streams, and rocky ledges, until you see Lake Skannatati once again, this time on your right. It seems peaceful and inviting, as you wind your way back toward the parking area.

After the Walk

You might be interested in visiting a restored blast furnace from the heyday of the iron mining era: the Clove Furnace Historic Site, once called Greenwood Furnace, then Arden Furnace. The operation began in 1854, to make iron for Civil War cannons. It thrived until 1885, when it was converted to a dairy farm. This site includes a number of buildings from its various lives, among them the impressive furnace itself, two stone silos from the place's farm days, a quaint but run-down farm building that was once a milk bottling factory, and the turbine building that provided power to operate it. You can walk around the structure and wind your way up a little hill to reach the top, from where the iron ore, limestone, and other necessary ingredients were dumped into the ironworks.

The furnace is open Monday through Friday, from 8:00 A.M. to noon and 1:00 to 5:00 P.M. For further information call the Orange County Historical Society at (845) 351–4696. To reach the Clove Furnace: After you leave the parking lot at Lake Skannatati, retrace your route north on Seven Lakes Drive. At Tiorati Circle take Arden Valley Road west to Route 17. Turn right (north) on 17 for about 1 mile. The furnace will be on your right.

30 | Autumn Apple Picking in an Orchard

Warwick

How to Get There: From uptown Manhattan, take the Major Deegan Expressway to the New York State Thruway north, across the Tappan Zee Bridge to exit 16. Take Route 17 west to exit 127 and head south on Route 13, which is also called Kings Highway. Three miles south of the town of Sugar Loaf, make a right turn at Four Corners Road and follow the signs for Applewood Orchards and Winery.

On a crisp autumn day, one of our favorite walks is through the orderly rows of apple-laden trees in David Hull's Applewood Orchards and Winery. These 160 acres of rolling orchard hillside with distant valley views are an inviting spot for strolling at will, picking apples (several kinds), and admiring the Grandma Moses–style scene. This is also a winery, with tastings and other events (for information visit www.applewoodorchardandwinery .com). A small pond, picnic tables, and brilliant red apples weighing down the trees give this setting an old-fashioned American look and feel.

This orchard is one of several in the Warwick area, and its atmosphere makes it by far our favorite. The people who work there are friendly and invited us to wander as we wished. There were a minimum of "do" and "don't" signs (unlike a nearby orchard that forbids just about everything you can think of), and we felt entirely comfortable strolling off among the trees. In fact, the whole region around Applewood is a particularly nice one for wandering. The rolling hills, with their luxuriant

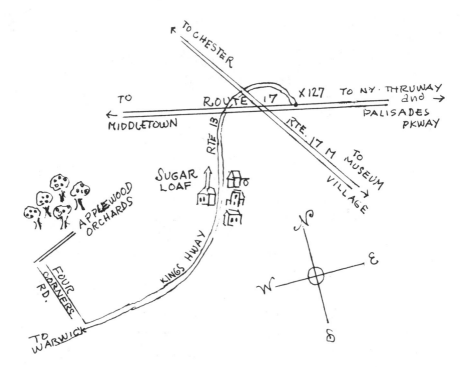

fall foliage, and the meadows filled with autumn wildflowers in delicate lavenders and shades of gold make the area look like a picture postcard. There are many nature walks in the vicinity, and only 3 miles from the orchard is Sugar Loaf, a charming craft village (see below).

While autumn is the obvious time to wander through an orchard and to bring home its bounty, we also recommend blossom time in the spring for pure beauty. The orchard is open spring, summer and fall, seven days a week, from 9:00 A.M. to 5:00 P.M. This is the perfect family outing, not only because children and adults find apple-picking fun, but also because the gentle slopes, dozens of grassy lanes between the trees, and fresh clean air make walking very easy. There are tractor and wagon rides, too, for those who don't want to stroll. You can phone the orchard at (914) 986–1684 for more information.

The Walk

When you arrive at Applewood, you'll see a small barn where you can pick up empty apple bags and a map of the orchard, as well as farm produce. The map lays out the area of the orchard, including where to find trees of MacIntosh, Cortland, Rome Beauty, Red Delicious, and Golden Delicious apples. You can either plot your route according to the kinds of apples you like, or head down the driveway to the oldest house in Orange County, the Staats House, which was built in 1700 and is at one end of the orchard, and start from there. Stopping for a look over the valley below, you can begin your stroll in the Rome Beauty section of the orchard, and proceed along, plucking apples off the trees as you wish. (Apple pickers—long-handled baskets—are for rent if you're serious about reaching the high ones.) Either walk straight through the orchard, or zig and zag as you wish, ending up at the pond that we found nestled below the trees and surrounded with children who had just come from a tractor ride through the orchard. The man in the barn will estimate the weight of your bag of apples and charge you (very reasonably). If you have picked no apples, that's all right, too.

After the Walk

We have already mentioned Sugar Loaf, and it is indeed a special spot to visit. Known as the "Village of Craftsmen," the tiny settlement includes more than a dozen crafts workshops and galleries, and you can watch the making of candles, jewelry, stained glass, and rag dolls. Sculptors, instrument makers, quilters, and other artists were at work when we were there. For information and special events at Sugar Loaf, call (845) 469–9181.

Not far away, on Route 17 at exit 129, is the Museum Village of Orange County (845–782–8247), a large outdoor museum with more than thirty buildings housing demonstrations of crafts and early-American life. After your morning at the apple orchard, these two sites will fit right into your country outing.

31 | A Romantic Riverside Walk
Nyack Beach State Park, Nyack

How to Get There: From the George Washington Bridge, take the Palisades Interstate Parkway to exit 4. Go north on Route 9W about 9 miles to Nyack Beach State Park. (After about 5.5 miles you come to a blinker light. Bear right, take Broadway, and keep going straight, past the village of Nyack. You will run right into the park. Take the road to the right, down the hill, to the parking area.)

This is a beautiful, romantic riverside walk in which the Hudson River is so close, you can actually put your feet in at any moment. The winding path is a one-way trail along the riverbank, but you will find it interesting and varied even when you retrace your steps. The red sandstone, shale, and traprock cliffs of the Palisades at Hook Mountain border the trail on one side, while the gently lapping river flanks the other.

The trail is totally flat, with occasional picnic tables and lookout rocks. You can go 1.7 miles to the end or do any part of it, remembering that you have to walk back. This is an all-season walk, though it can be cold and blustery in winter. However, many particularly enjoy it then, when large ice floes dot the river and bang up against the shoreline. Even on the hottest summer days, the walk is pleasant, breezy, and partly shaded. In late spring you will find a wonderful variety of wildflowers. As might be expected, Sundays are more crowded, although we have never found it unpleasantly so. The rest of the time it is a mostly quiet, solitary walk.

We recommend this outing for anyone, including families with children. But remember that young children must be kept from the temptation of climbing too high up on the rocky outcroppings. Elderly walkers will love this cool, breezy trail.

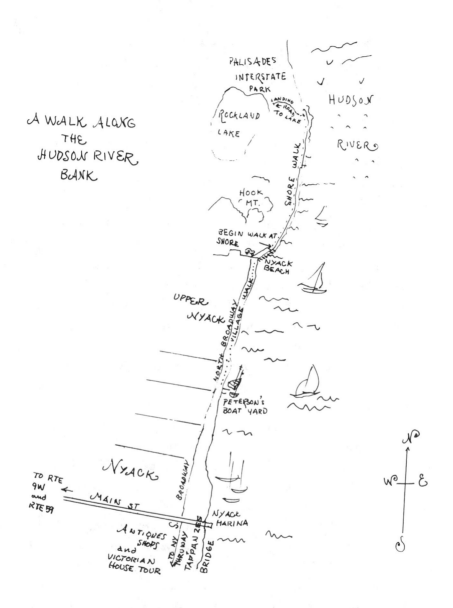

A WALK ALONG
THE
HUDSON RIVER
BANK

PALISADES
INTERSTATE
PARK

ROCKLAND
LAKE

HUDSON

LANDING
& ROAD
TO LAKE

RIVER

SHORE WALK

HOOK
MT.

BEGIN WALK AT
SHORE

NYACK
BEACH

UPPER
NYACK

NORTH BROADWAY VILLAGE WALK

PETERSON'S
BOAT YARD

NYACK

TO RTE
9W
and
RTE 59

MAIN ST

BROADWAY

NYACK
MARINA

ANTIQUES SHOPS
and
VICTORIAN
HOUSE TOUR

TO NY
THRUWAY
TAPPAN ZEE
BRIDGE

N
W — E
S

Bring a picnic, as there are no concessions along the way. Any good, comfortable shoes will do, since you will find the path soft and easy on the feet. This is a fine walk for picture-taking or sketching, with the ever-changing river at your side. Some people ride bikes on the trail, while others bring their dogs.

Nyack Beach State Park is open daily from 8:00 A.M. until dusk. There is a small parking fee in season. For information call (845) 268–3020.

The Walk

Leave your car in the parking area by the river, and head north on the narrow cinder trail before you.

If you're here in late spring, you'll enjoy the array of wildflowers and plants that flank the path on both sides: wild geraniums, roses, daisies, honeysuckle, wild grape, tall grasses that bend with gentle breezes. There are dramatic clusters of rocks along the mountainside forming majestic cliffs that dominate the landscape. These steep cliffs were quarried in the late nineteenth century to provide rock for growing New York City. Some thirty-two quarries cut rock from sites along here; it was then barged down the river to the city.

At every bend you will come to great river views. Take your binoculars and observe life on the water. On Sundays sailboat races are often held, and occasionally you'll spot a Hudson River schooner sailing by. Across the water you can see the historic sites of Washington Irving lore: Philipse Manor and Sleepy Hollow Manor and the village of Ossining, with its formidable Sing Sing prison. To the north you might see Croton, if it's a clear day, and Croton Point Park jutting out into the river. On the river itself, in addition to the passing boats, you might spot a variety of ducks or geese lazily swimming by. Occasionally you'll cross a hidden path going up the hill to the left into Hook Mountain State Park, but we suggest you stay on the main trail, which is the most scenic.

After about a mile you will reach an especially attractive lookout point. If you've taken your dog (they are allowed here as long as they are leashed), this is a good place to let it wade into the Hudson. You can stop and rest at one of the picnic tables here and take in the view.

If you continue north, you will come to Landing Road, a fairly steep paved road to the left, which will take you into Rockland Lake State Park (see Outing 26). This marks the end of our walk, although you may wish to continue. If you do go on, after about five minutes you will see a smaller paved path to the right, which goes back down to the river, then north, paralleling the river for several more miles to the town of Haverstraw. On your return you will have the Tappan Zee Bridge before you, as a focus for your walk.

After the Walk

If you're not too tired, you might wish to explore further. From the parking area walk back up the paved road and reenter the park, going uphill this time, to the wonderful plateau of Hook Mountain. There are playing fields, more picnic tables, and views galore. This is a great spot for children!

If you are still in the mood for more activity, drive to the village of Nyack, now quite an antiques center. Most of the antiques (and crafts) shops are located on South Broadway from Depew Avenue to Main Street, though there are some on Main Street as well. Sundays are fairly busy, when tourists and collectors arrive en masse. Those who prefer ambling at a more leisurely pace would enjoy strolling through the village during the week; most of the shops are open Tuesday through Sunday.

In addition, we suggest you at least catch a glimpse of the following:

In Upper Nyack, on your way south from the park, stop and look at the Old Stone Church, the oldest in Rockland County, dating from 1813. The church is located on North Broadway near Birchwood.

Petersen's Boatyard on Van Houten Street, off North Broadway, has been functioning since 1898. Although there are no boat rentals, it's fun to browse around.

The Edward Hopper House, at 82 North Broadway (845–358–0774), is the boyhood home of the artist Edward Hopper. Built in 1858, it is now a small art gallery that shows works by Rockland County artists. The Hopper House provides short walking tour maps of some of the local places Hopper knew and painted.

Nyack has some special events that might interest you. There are two annual street fairs, in May and September, featuring arts, crafts, and antiques, when many dealers set up shop on the streets in town. Call (845) 268–3888 for information. On Thursdays, from early June until Thanksgiving, there is an open-air farmers' market in the municipal parking lot in the center of town at Main and Cedar Streets. Here you will find fresh-picked produce. It's best to get there early (soon after 8:30 A.M.), as the market is very popular.

Nearby
Connecticut

32 | A Quaint New England Village
Litchfield

How to Get There: From the west side of Manhattan, take the Henry Hudson Parkway (West Side Highway) to the Saw Mill River Parkway, to Interstate 684 north, to Interstate 84 east. Take exit 17 and go north on Connecticut Route 63 to Litchfield. From the east side of Manhattan, take F.D.R. Drive to the Major Deegan Expressway, to the Saw Mill River Parkway, and follow the same directions as above.

This is a trip to a rare, unspoiled New England town. Litchfield is a village that has managed to retain its colonial character for almost 300 years. The visitor arriving here is astonished by the seemingly endless rows of perfect eighteenth-century white houses, the elegant Congregational Church poised above the town green, the cobblestone courtyards of shops. But Litchfield is not a reconstruction or a self-conscious preservation effort; it has been able to retain its architectural integrity by vigilant citizen effort and through accidents of geography and history. Yet it is a bustling town with lots to see within a relatively concentrated area.

Litchfield has an illustrious history for such a small place. It was home to the nation's first law school and the first seminary for girls, and the eighteenth-century home of Connecticut's chief justice is found here as well as the 1787 parsonage where Harriet Beecher Stowe's father lived. Litchfield was a small but well-to-do colonial and federalist settlement, as can be seen from the grandeur of its early homes.

In 1719 Litchfield was incorporated in the Connecticut Assembly, divided into sixty homesteads each of fifteen acres.

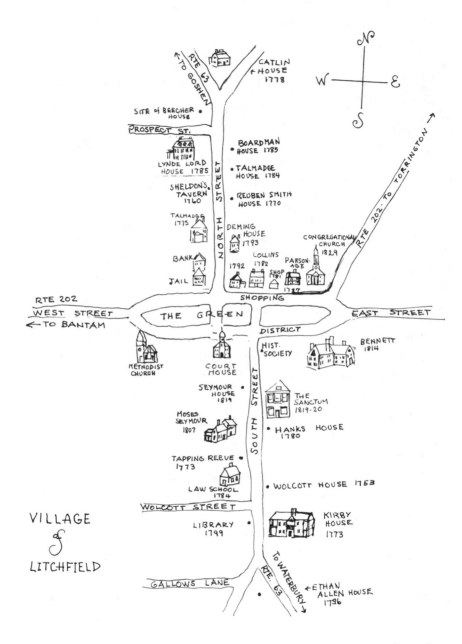

VILLAGE
of
LITCHFIELD

Some of these can still be visited. The colonists prospered, and soon Litchfield became an important stagecoach stop between Boston and New York, and Albany and New Haven. In 1751 it was chosen to be county seat. By the time of the Revolution, Litchfield, strongly on the patriot side, provided as many as 500 men to the effort. Among the Revolutionary tales is one describing how an equestrian statue of George III was toppled in New York City and dragged all the way to Oliver Wolcott's woodshed on South Street in Litchfield, where it was melted down into bullets by the local ladies. And, we should add, both Lafayette and Washington slept here—many times.

Litchfield citizens became prominent in several fields. Tapping Reeve (not an original landowner) started the nation's first law school in 1774; among its students were Aaron Burr (Reeve's brother-in-law), twenty-eight senators, three Supreme Court justices, and more than a hundred congressmen. Here Sarah Pierce opened her Female Academy, the first school for young ladies' higher education in the country.

By the 1850s, when railroads brought people and prosperity to towns along their lines, Litchfield was left behind. In 1859 it was still the only four-horse stagecoach stop on the Naugatuck Road. As it escaped industrialization, it became a haven for retired people, summer visitors, and eventually for commuters attracted by the quiet charms of the village and surrounding hills. In 1913 the White Memorial Foundation incorporated to preserve the area, including Bantam Lake; some 5,000 acres are devoted to a bird sanctuary, wild gardens, and recreational facilities. And in 1959 Litchfield itself was designated a historic area. Tapping Reeve's law school and the village green, as well as areas of both North and South Streets, are registered National Historic Sites.

For your walk you need not bring anything but comfortables shoes and an interest in architecture, crafts shops, and Americana. Pick up a walking tour map at the information center on the village green for a detailed guide to each house. A colonial architecture guide is a good idea if you're interested in such details as eaves, roof lines, and fan windows.

The Fall Foliage Rally, held at White Memorial Foundation on a Sunday in early October, is an event children will especially enjoy. Horses and ponies pull carriages and wagons in a series of races. Children are welcome to ask for free rides between competitions. Call (860) 354–6507 for information. The annual tour of selected historic houses occurs on the second Saturday of July (for a small fee). Call the chamber of commerce at (860) 482–6586 for details.

The Walk

A first glimpse will make you want to explore all of this picture-postcard New England village—its village green, broad tree-lined avenues, and charming side streets. The historic district lies right in the center of town along the green and North and South Streets, which are each about a half mile long. As mentioned before, we suggest stopping by the information center on the village green to pick up a map. You will walk past stately colonial homes, uniformly white with black shutters, that have been occupied by governors, justices, and senators through the years, as well as the birthplaces of Ethan Allen, Henry Ward Beecher, and Harriet Beecher Stowe.

Your walk should begin with the church at the green. The first Congregational Church is a fine example of the double octagon steeple design. Built in 1829, it was moved in the 1870s; after functioning as a meeting place and movie house, in 1929 it was returned to its proper site on the green. Proceed along the green by the parsonage (1787), past three small shops from the 1780s, and then north along North Street. At the watering trough, cross the street and start back on the other side, passing five homes, Sheldon's Tavern (another spot where George Washington actually slept), the bank, and the jail. At the green are the Methodist Church and the Court House.

Along South Street you will find the Tapping Reeve House (1773) and many other interesting sites:

The Litchfield Historical Society and Museum (203–567–5862) in the Noyes Memorial Building exhibits Revolutionary period paintings, including those of Ralph Earl, as well as some furniture and law books, in an uncluttered and inviting setting. Open April through December, Tuesday through Saturday, from 11:00 A.M. to 5:00 P.M. Cobble Court, around the corner from the Historical Society, is a well-appointed group of small shops featuring local handcrafts, clothing, imported yarns, new and old books, and cookware.

Tapping Reeve House and Law School, South Street, graduated over 1,000 notable students who contributed greatly to American society, such as Horace Mann, Aaron Burr, and John C. Calhoun. Inside the museum, dedicated to Judge Reeve, you can see fine antique furniture that belonged to the Reeve family and sundry historic mementoes. The tiny schoolhouse next door has on display handwritten ledgers of students and original law books. You can visit from May through October, 11:00 A.M. to 5:00 P.M.

Wolcott Memorial Library, South Street, exhibits paintings, sculptures, and photography. Though the main library is new, it is attached to a 1799 house built by Oliver Wolcott Jr., son of one of the signers of the Declaration of Independence. Open year-round, Tuesday through Saturday.

After the Walk

Within easy driving distance you'll find several unusual places to visit:

Haight Vineyards and Winery, Chestnut Hill Road, Litchfield (860–567–4045), is an unusual fifteen-acre farm winery operated by a small staff using traditional methods. Tours and tastings are offered free of charge Wednesday through Saturday from 10:30 A.M. to 4:30 P.M.

White Flower Farm, Route 63 in Morris (860–567–8789), is a beautiful nursery that attracts visitors from considerable distances because of its unusual assortment of plants. Open April through November, its gardens and greenhouses are particularly lovely in late spring and summer.

If you still have energy to spare, you might want to drive to nearby Washington, a hilltop community with wonderful views over miles of valleys with rolling hills, or New Preston and Washington Depot, which are also worth a detour.

White Memorial Foundation and Litchfield Nature Center, off Route 202 west of Litchfield (860–567–0857), is a 4,000-acre nature center and wildlife preserve—the largest in the state-that is particularly popular with birders. With its eleven ponds and the Bantam River, the preserve provides just the right type of environment for over 200 species: grackles, starlings, bluebirds, woodpeckers, goldfinches, crows, owls, and wading birds (including herons), to name a few. You can watch birds from a special observatory where you cannot be seen by them.

33 | A Revolutionary War Encampment Site
Putnam Memorial State Park, Redding

How to Get There: From the east side of Manhattan, take F.D.R. Drive to the Major Deegan Expressway, to the Cross County Parkway east, to the Hutchinson River Parkway north, to the Merritt Parkway, to exit 45 (Connecticut Route 58). Follow Route 58 north for 13.8 miles to its intersection with Route 107. The historic park is on your left where you see the statue. You can leave your car along the side of the road near the entrance.

In 1778–79 General Israel Putnam and his troops of the Continental Army braved the Connecticut winter on this wooded, stony hillside. The encampment made use of the natural caves and protection afforded by the giant boulders, a freshwater spring, and the lookouts over the countryside below. The site still contains the remains of chimneys, the foundations of the officers' huts, and several small reconstructed buildings, which give the visitor the feeling of the time and place. And the natural setting is unusually pretty, with a sparkling lake and fine views, not much different from what they must have been when the sentries looked out over the wooded hillsides for marauding Tories.

If you are a history buff, this is an especially nice way to enjoy the rock-strewn Connecticut countryside. We relished the fresh crisp air on the hillside and the nice trails, as well as the feeling of walking in the Continental Army's campsite. We recommend this outing for families with children, particularly if they are old enough to enjoy the historical significance and strong enough to scamper over the many rock formations and rather steep hillside.

There are two parts to this park: one, with the campsite features, is not too large and on the hill; the other is quite flat, around the wooded Lake Putnam, where any walker can easily find a nice trail.

This is one of the oldest state parks in Connecticut. About a hundred years after the original encampment, it became a memorial park, and additions have been made at various times since then. Unlike so many "official" historic sites, this one has a very natural look, though there has been some reconstruction. There is a distinctive statue at the entrance, showing General Putnam riding his horse down steps cut into a cliffside. Made by Anna Hyatt Huntington when she was in her nineties, it sets the tone for the park: It is dignified and heroic, but on a small scale, as were so many battles and encampments of the Revolution.

Within the park is a small museum, the Revolutionary War Museum, open daily from May 15 to September 15, 9:00 A.M. to 5:00 P.M., and weekends until October 15. It has a nice collection of historical material and a map of the parkland. The park itself is open all year for walking, as are the little hut and reconstruction of the soldiers' living quarters (some eight to twelve men slept in this tiny, windowless building). Of course, you can view the various pits and foundations at any time. For information call (203) 938–2285.

This is a good outing for a picnic. There are no concession booths or commercial establishments, though there are restrooms. You are, of course, only a mile or two from the towns of Bethel and Redding, where you can get refreshments at a number of places, but the lookouts and picnic areas near the lake are ideal for eating alfresco. You might also want to take your binoculars, as there are great views and many birds, including hummingbirds in fall migration. Wear good walking shoes or sneakers if you plan to climb over rocks.

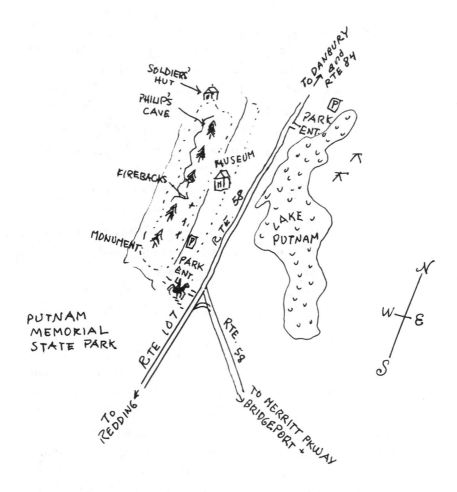

The Walk

Park near the entrance to the campsite where you see the Huntington statue and pick up a map and historical material at the small museum near the gate. The first things you see that suggest the encampment are piles of stones along the edge of the road. These are the remains of the fireplaces and chimneys of the wooden huts of the soldiers. They give an uncanny feeling of the past. As you walk along the bottom of the hillside, you will come to a dirt path where you'll find an entire chimney from one of the soldiers' huts. If you follow the main roadway, you'll spot a large rocky configuration with steps and railing built alongside. Here natural protection from rain, wind, and snow was afforded the troops by hollows in the rocks and shallow caves. One such cave is called Philip's cave; there is a local legend that after the Revolution a soldier named Philip returned to live there. On your right you'll see a reconstructed officers' barrack, a dark windowless shack with a dirt floor.

There are several small paths leading into the woods, which will bring you to lookouts or foundations of other buildings. You'll also find a burial monument to the fifteen soldiers who died during the encampment, and a stone-lined magazine, where gunpowder or munitions were probably stored. Among these sites are stands of larch, or tamarack, our only deciduous conifer. In the autumn the needles are golden before they fall, giving the hillside a beautiful glow.

When you have completed your tour, you can return to your car and drive up the road a short distance, this time turning to the right. Here is the adjoining part of Putnam Memorial State Park. It surrounds Lake Putnam, a breathtaking lake with lotus and water lilies floating on it. There are picnic facilities in this part of the park and several pretty nature trails. You can find further signs of the encampment here: both fireback remains and a freshwater spring that probably supplied the soldiers with water.

After the Walk

You are in an unusually pretty area of Connecticut, with pleasant and scenic drives. For something unusual, visit the Bethel Firefighters Museum, at 36–40 South Street in Bethel.

34 | The "Jewel of Long Island Sound"
Southport

How to Get There: From the west side of Manhattan, take the Henry Hudson Parkway (West Side Highway) to the Cross Bronx Expressway, to Interstate 95 north, to exit 19. Follow the signs to Southport. From the east side of Manhattan, take F.D.R. Drive to the Major Deegan Expressway, to Interstate 278 to I–95, and follow the same directions as above.

This elegant little village, with its scenic harbor on the Sound, is about an hour away from New York City. It is ideal for strolling, with its pleasant winding roads and salt smell of the sea. You're never more than several blocks from the water. Impeccable nineteenth-century homes and fine old trees line the streets; its historic district was the first designated in Connecticut. Unlike more bustling waterfront communities such as nearby Fairfield, Southport seems to sit firmly in the nineteenth century. It has been able to resist commercial expansion and to retain an unusually peaceful flavor.

The Indians sold their claims to Southport in 1661 for "13 coats, two yards apiece, and ye rest in wampum." "Mill River," as it was then called, was at first a prosperous farming area. It began to develop into a village around the time its shipyard was built in 1763. Its natural harbor was small but deep enough to handle one brig. There are still some buildings left from this period. Along Harbor Road you can see several old warehouses that have been converted to residences. In addition, you should note the Gurdon Perry House (circa 1830) at 780 Harbor Road and the Austin Perry House (circa 1830) at 712 Harbor Road.

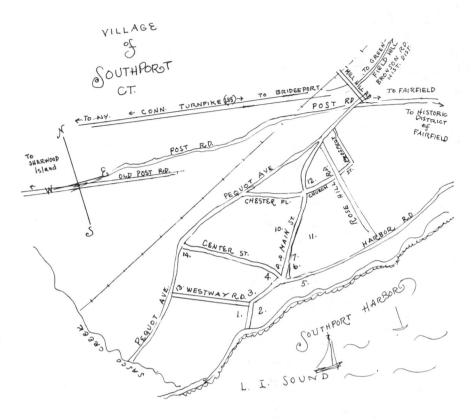

Soon the town and harbor were growing rapidly and becoming so prosperous that some of the residents even had their own fleets of vessels that sailed to far-off places in the Orient, Europe, or South America. Onion farming was developed in the nineteenth century and eventually became the town's main source of wealth, bringing the village the nickname "onion capital of America." Southport onions even helped prevent scurvy among the troops during the Civil War.

In the late nineteenth century, the town began to attract New Yorkers looking for a pleasant place to spend the summer. Several fine mansions, as well as the Romanesque-style Pequot Library, date from the Victorian period. Southport became an affluent residential suburb, as new estates were built in the

Green Farms and Sasco Hill areas. The Pequot Yacht Club became (and remains) the center of the harbor front.

If you enjoy strolling through lanes of graceful old houses with widow's walks amid gentle seaside breezes, you'll like this outing. A history of Southport called "Walking Through History" is available at the Fairfield Historic Society in Fairfield.

Southport is a relatively uncommercial town, although there are a few shops and a variety or restaurants. Or, we recommend driving to Jennings Beach in Fairfield for a picnic right on the Sound. (Bring your bathing suit!)

You can easily do this outing in an hour or so, and anyone seeking a real Yankee seaside village walk will enjoy Southport. It's easy on the feet and the energy and relatively simple to reach. Since the boating and swimming facilities are not available to visitors (unless, of course, you arrive by boat), it may be frustrating to small children—even if you promise to go swimming or sailing later.

We recommend that you visit in summer, although spring and fall are lovely too. A couple of special events that might persuade you to go at a particular time include the Dogwood Festival, which takes place in the nearby town of Greenfield Hill (Old Academy and Bronson Roads). The festival is a weeklong celebration featuring the 30,000 dogwoods, some of which were originally transplanted after the Revolution. It takes place under a tent on the green and features concerts, art shows, sales, and walking tours. Call (203) 259–2128 for the exact date and/or luncheon reservations. Fairfield Day is celebrated at Jennings Beach on the last Sunday in June, when the town sponsors children's races, egg throwing, musical entertainment, clowns, and even a sky-diving exhibition. No admission charge; arrive before 11:00 A.M. to avoid traffic and parking problems. Call (203) 367–8495 for further information.

The Walk

In addition to the buildings listed below, you should visit the harbor, the focal point of the village. Put your feet in the water! Just viewing Long Island Sound from the coast of Connecticut is a pleasure on a nice day. Southport and some of its surrounding villages have nice waterfronts for watching tides change, boats coming and going, or gulls soaring overhead. Look for seaweed, barnacles, mussels, clams, and other marine life along the sandy coast of the Sound. Gulls and waterfowl abound.

For the walk through town, start at the corner of Westway and Harbor Roads. (Numbers are keyed to map.)

1. William Bulkley House (circa 1760) at 824 Harbor Road is one of the oldest houses still standing on Southport harbor. It is called a "three-quarters house," meaning that there are four bay windows in the front instead of the more usual five. The house has recently been restored.

2. Old storehouses (early nineteenth century) at 789 and 825 Harbor Road have been converted to residences. Number 789 was also used as a clubhouse for the Pequot Yacht Club.

3. Gurdon Perry House (circa 1830) at 780 Harbor Road belonged to a wealthy merchant in the early part of the nineteenth century. An unpretentious house, it is simpler in style than many later homes built for merchants.

4. Austin Perry House (circa 1830) at 712 Harbor Road is particularly interesting for its portico, which is considered one of the finest of its kind, probably dating from the 1840s.

5. Pequot Yacht Club (circa 1835) at 669 Harbor Road was a warehouse during the port's commercial peak.

6. Jennings Store Building (circa 1834 and later) at 668–70 Harbor Road included the town's first general store and post office. Sections were added during the Victorian period, when the second floor was used as a reading room before the Pequot Library was built.

7. Southport National Bank (1833) at 227 Main Street is now a private residence. Note its Greek Revival style.
8. Hall block and chronicle buildings (1894) at 244 and 252 Main Street were once tenements that housed stores and offices. They were converted into apartments in the 1950s.
9. Southport Savings Bank (1865) at 226 Main Street was built to resemble the roof pitch of the Trinity Episcopal Church.
10. Oliver Bulkley House (1859) at 176 Main Street is a wonderful example of early Gothic architecture. For some years this house was called the Pequot Inn; it was used by summer boarders in the 1920s until it was converted into a private home. Note its lovely grounds.
11. Charles M. Gilman House (1873) at 139 Main Street is an interesting combination of Italianate and Gothic styles.
12. Old Academy (1827) at 95 Main Street has served in many capacities. First a private school, it then held church services, and finally became a private home in the late nineteenth century.
13. Pequot Library (circa 1894), located at the intersection of Westway Road and Pequot Avenue, was designed by a student of H. H. Richardson in Romanesque style and donated to the village.
14. Trinity Episcopal Church (1862), on the corner of Pequot Avenue and Center Street, was built in the Carpenter Gothic style after its original structure (virtually identical) was destroyed by a tornado. The church has a lovely slender spire that can be seen for miles.

After the Walk

There are many odd and amusing places in the vicinity of Southport. Jennings Beach (off Fairfield Beach Road in Fairfield), a wide expanse of nice sandy beach with pleasantly choppy seas, is well worth a visit. The Birdcraft Museum, 314 Uniquowa Road, Fairfield, has a collection of 2,000 mounted birds and mammal specimens on display, as well as some 50 decoys. The Old Burying Ground in Fairfield has many pre-Revolutionary gravestones, some carved with angels, skulls, or willows. Bring your own grave-rubbing materials, or pick some up at the several art supply stores in Fairfield. The cemetery is located along Beach Road.

Sherwood Island is a state-owned facility off Westport with large bathhouses, just west of Southport (the quickest route is back onto Interstate 95 to the Sherwood Island exit and across the causeway to the beach). It is somewhat crowded in season.

The P. T. Barnum Museum, 820 Main Street in Bridgeport, dedicated to the great circus showman, is fun, from the curiosities inside—such as a 50,000-piece model circus and Tom Thumb memorabilia—to the architecture itself, with its dome-shaped and "eyebrow" dormers. If you're a circus fan, this flamboyant museum is a good stop. To get there, take I–95 to exit 27 and turn toward downtown Bridgeport and Main Street.

35 | Home and Studio of J. Alden Weir

Weir Farm, Ridgefield

How to Get There: Weir Farm is located in southwestern Connecticut in the towns of Ridgefield and Wilton. From the east side of Manhattan, take F.D.R. Drive to the Major Deegan Expressway, to the Cross County Parkway east, the Hutchinson River Parkway north, to the Merritt Parkway, to Route 7 north, through Wilton and Branchville. Go left on Route 102 and take the second road on your left, Old Branchville Road; turn left on Nod Hill Road to Weir Farm. The Weir Preserve is entered at either Pelham Lane or Nod Hill Road; signs are posted.

Western Connecticut is an area of gentle hills, stone walls, fine old oak trees, and red barns. Its rolling landscape is tranquil and picturesque, rather than dramatic. It is the kind of place that is inviting for walkers, particularly at its greenest, in late spring or summer, when the light and the colors seem wonderfully fresh.

Some time after dozens of painters had begun flocking to Giverny in France to learn about impressionism from the master, Claude Monet, a small but significant group of American artists, led by J. Alden Weir, started painting outdoors in Connecticut, taking the first steps toward American impressionism.

Weir had aquired an old farm in Branchville (now part of Ridgefield) in 1882. With his colleague John Twachtman and many friends, including John Singer Sargent, Childe Hassam, and Albert Pinkham Ryder, Weir explored the Connecticut landscape. Weir and Twachtman began painting outdoors, examining the effect of light on color—taking the first gentle steps toward the European style of impressionism. Weir Farm, recently dedicated as a National Historic Site, the first national park in Connecticut, was the scene of robust artistic activity from the 1880s until Weir's death in 1919. Its studios and surrounding landscape (a delightful stroll covering sixty-two acres) were saved from development at the last minute. Though the farm has shrunk from its original 238 acres, it is still large enough to include many a picturesque landscape, and even a lily pond that Weir built, perhaps with Giverny in mind.

In order to fully appreciate the setting, however, a little bit of art history might be welcome, for Weir Farm was—in its simple, picturesque way—an important location in the development of American painting.

J. Alden Weir, the son of a drawing professor at West Point, Robert Weir (who taught both Generals Grant and Lee, by the way), and younger brother of landscapist John Ferguson Weir, was for many years a conservative, academic painter. When he went off as a young man to study art in Paris, he wrote back in 1877: "I went across the river the other day to see an exhibition of the work of a new school who call themselves 'Impressionists.' I never in my life saw more horrible things. They do not observe drawing nor form but give you an impression of what they call nature." Weir came from an academic artistic background, painting realistic topographic scenes, and giving drawing and form major importance in his compositions. The hazy impressionistic painting that he saw abroad opposed the principles with which he had come to Europe. He shared America's anti-European feeling about "foreign" styles of art, though he—like all young artists—went to Europe for traditional art study.

On his return to the United States, Weir settled in New York, where he was a successful painter of delicate, naturalistic still lifes, flower pieces, portraits, and domestic scenes. But Weir was a great nature lover, having been raised on Emerson and "back to nature" themes. In 1883 he moved his family to the farm in Connecticut to escape urban life; soon the beauty

WEIR FARM

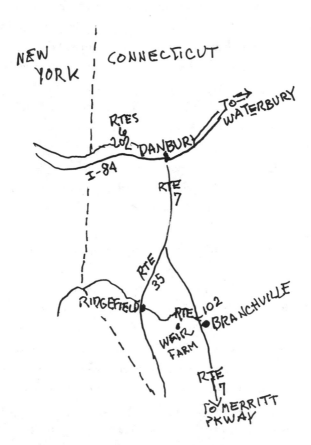

of his surroundings beckoned him to begin painting outdoors. Before long, Weir—a gregarious, magnetic figure in the art world—had brought other painters to his home in Branchville. He was to paint there every summer for thirty-seven years. By 1890 he and Twachtman were experimenting with impressionistic scenes on the farm, using color to create the sense of flickering light and subtle changes in the light throughout the day.

They became so excited by outdoor painting that they even devised a portable winter studio. (You can see the sites of these forays on the farm when you visit.)

Weir went on to organize and guide the Ten, a loosely knit but nonetheless influential group of American impressionists. Their collective withdrawal from the established exhibitions in New York to show their works together was a revolutionary moment in American painting. But Weir and his colleagues did not consider themselves rebels. They never abandoned entirely their American roots; American impressionism retained an interest in subject matter and the factual (though Weir never minded adding or transposing a tree or flower—he called it "hollyhocking"). Their paintings and explorations of light were an outgrowth of the luminist tradition in American art, and they saw their experiments in painting light as a natural step forward. They never issued a manifesto of impressionism, nor sought to make dramatic political statements. Both Weir and Twatchman, as well as their colleagues the Ten, were somewhat surprised by their designation as American impressionists.

Weir Farm became a center for artists, and Weir himself held open-air classes. Nearby Cos Cob soon became an art colony, where his friends took summer homes. Weir was a busy man, painting, teaching, encouraging, and supporting his colleagues, and serving on the board of the Metropolitan Museum of Art and as president of the National Academy of Design. His personal charm and dynamism (he was known as "the diplomat") enabled him to move the static world of academic art forward, without dramatic means or revolutionary art.

Weir lived at the farm until his death. His daughter Dorothy, also a painter, married the sculptor Mahonri Young, who built the second studio and continued to work there.

The Walk

Today, Weir Farm is managed by the National Park Service and the Weir Farm Trust. For operating hours and seasons, visit online at www.nps.gov/wefa/pphtm/planyourvisit/html, or call 203–834–1896 for an appointment. Visitors can explore Weir Farm and partake in a variety of art-related programs and activities for kids—you can even set up an easel on the grounds and paint your own "impressions" of the landscape. The Park Service and the Trust offer tours, exhibitions, and art classes for children. The Trust also offers Visiting Artist and Artist-in-Residence programs.

The grounds are open for walking, and there's an Art Explorer's Trail that takes you past some of Weir's favorite painting spots. You can also tour Weir's studio, built in 1885 and heated by a potbellied stove. The interior is still much as it was in Weir's day, with its clutter of brushes, paints, canvas, and other artifacts belonging to the artist; there's also a printing press (Weir was also an etcher) and even a painting on Weir's old easel. Plan to visit Weir Farm on a day when the studio is open.

You will also find a nature preserve adjacent to the farm. The Weir Preserve consists of 110 additional acres of unspoiled Connecticut landscape given by the artist's daughter and several other residents of the area. A map with listings of wildflowers and trees is available at Weir Farm.

After the Walk

For a complete change of pace, visit the nearby Aldrich Museum of Contemporary Art at 258 Main Street in Ridgefield. This attractive museum is particularly noted for its modern sculpture garden and for its very trendy changing exhibitions. Without visiting the Chelsea galleries in New York, you can get a taste of the latest avant-garde paintings, sculpture, constructions, and conceptual art.

Using a map given at the desk, you can spot large works in the outdoor sculpture collection by Tony Rosenthal, Arnaldo Pomodoro, Robert Morris, Lila Katzen, David Von Schlagel, Sol LeWitt, Alexander Liberman, and other contemporary sculptors and construction artists. There is an entrance fee for the museum, but the sculpture garden can be seen separately without going indoors. Telephone (203) 438–4519 for hours and information on new exhibitions.

Nearby
Pennsylvania

36 | A Medicinal Trail Walk

Bowman's Hill State Wildflower Preserve, Washington's Crossing

How to Get There: Take the New Jersey Turnpike south to exit 9, then Route 1 south toward Trenton. Pick up Interstate 95/295 south after Princeton (at Bakersville), and take the interstate to the exit at Yardley, Pennsylvania. Turn back to Pennsylvania Route 32 and travel a few miles until you reach Bowman's Hill Preserve.

This unusual walk is along a trail devoted to plants that have real, or legendary, uses as medicines. A part of the lovely Bowman's Hill State Wildflower Preserve, the medicinal trail is a special outing for herb fanciers and those who are interested in natural curing or Indian herb uses. In our country the Indians often used herbal medicines, and modern science has frequently verified their effectiveness. Some have even been synthetically reproduced. Many plants are still used in pharmacology, but others are of no proven value—their curative properties are nothing more than old wives' tales. The medicinal trail includes some of each kind, with a descriptive flier that tells you what you're seeing and what it's good for—or what legends say it's good for.

The trail, which is about 620 feet long, is slow going, if you stop to examine each plant. While you are warned not to taste anything yourself—some of the plants are extremely poisonous—you are encouraged to go slowly and study each plant's story as you go. This outing, due to the dangerous nature of many of the plants, is not recommended for small children, particularly if you read the more disturbing legends aloud.

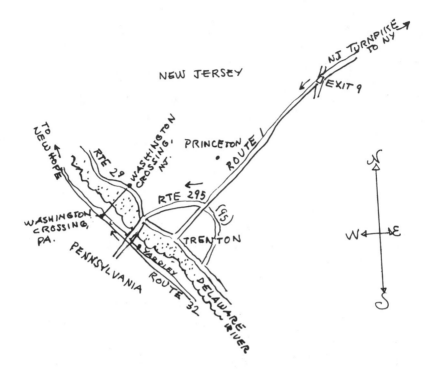

For other walks in Bowman's Hill State Wildflower Preserve,
see Outing 37, which can, of course, be combined with one walk
on the same day. There are a tree identification trail, wildflower
trails, and several kinds of nature walks in this preserve. Several
times during the year the preserve offers guided mushroom
walks, bird walks, and native plant and fern identification walks,
as well as other wild plant walks. The preserve is open year-
round, except for major holidays, and each season brings different plantings and appropriate events.

The Walk

The trail begins with mountain laurel, the juices of which the
Indians supposedly drank to commit suicide (but by 1800 a tinc-
ture made from its leaves was being used to treat several diseases).
Next comes mayapple and bloodroot, a source of morphine that

Indians chewed to cure a sore throat. Other plants include white oak, spicebush, wild ginger, alumroot, fairywand, and witch hazel. Among the old wives' varieties is ginseng, which Europeans thought restored youth (and which has been used for centuries as a cure-all in China). The list is a fairly long one, and a walk along these plants is extremely interesting.

After the Walk

See the suggestions following Outing 37.

37 | Exploring a Wildflower Preserve

Bowman's Hill State Wildflower Preserve, Washington's Crossing

How to Get There: Take the New Jersey Turnpike south to exit 9, then take Route 1 south toward Trenton. Pick up Interstate 95/295 south after Princeton (at Bakersville), and take the interstate to the exit at Yardley, Pennsylvania. Turn back to Pennsylvania Route 32. Bowman's Hill Preserve is several miles northwest on Route 32.

As you walk along the woodsy trails and gentle creek in this lovely spot, you'll feel you are miles from the bustle of the highway and civilization. The preserve has managed to include in its one hundred acres quite a variety of habitats—forest, meadows, ponds, bogs, an arboretum, and preserves for shrubs and flowers. An azalea trail leads to a path of bluebells; a marsh walk brings you to marigolds and holly areas; you pass the charming dam on Pidcock Creek and come to the evergreen area. The list is extensive, and the walk (quite hilly) is always interesting. You can choose your own paths—up and down and around about—with the help of a map and a variety of printed guides that are available near the parking area.

We found the preserve quite uninhabited in midsummer, but spring, with its profusion of wildflowers, is apt to be a bit busier. However, there is enough room for many visitors, and the trails are woodsy enough to absorb a fair number of people. The more energetic can hike to the famous Bowman's Hill Tower at the top of a surprisingly high hill in the preserve (or drive there), and complete their visit to this historic and lovely place.

Established to preserve Pennsylvania's native plants, Bowman's Hill opened in 1934. It is made up of twenty-six trails, including one that is wheelchair accessible, and a famous arboretum called Penn's Woods, which has more than 450 different trees and shrubs. The general atmosphere of Bowman's Hill Preserve is relaxed. It is rather like wandering through a large private nineteenth-century estate. There are few signs telling you what to do or not to do, and the fences and steps are made of natural materials that seem to have fallen in place by accident. The signs identifying the various walks and plants are almost hidden by foliage and are never obtrusive, so you don't feel as if you are in a preserve but in a series of natural habitats.

Pick up a guide to the various walks and a tree and flower guide to the preserve at the headquarters where you leave your car. You might want to take your own identifying books, too. Insect repellent, stout shoes, and a picnic are all recommended.

This walk, particularly if you climb to the lookout tower, can be rigorous. But if you want more gentle trails, the preserve has those as well. We recommend this outing for anyone who enjoys wildflowers, woods, and hiking. It is ideal for children, who can roam freely.

The preserve is open year-round, except for major holidays. Of course, wildflowers are best in spring and early summer, but there is something to be seen in any season.

The Walk

When you drive to Bowman's Hill Preserve, you will pass a picnic ground and public facilities near the entrance. Keep going and leave your car at the lot behind the headquarters. You can choose which of twenty-six trails you wish to set out on, but most run into one another and you can't go wrong whichever you take. If you go downhill from the parking lot, you will come to the creek, which you can follow along its winding path. If you

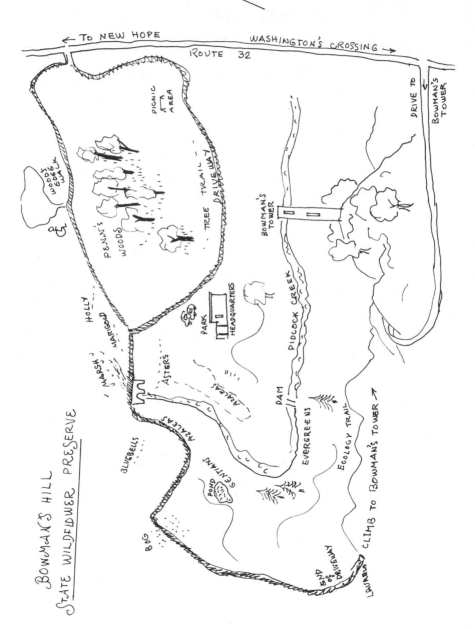

continue along the roadway (not accessible to cars) to its end, you will come to a rugged climb to Bowman's Tower. If you go back in the direction of the entrance, you can walk through the arboretum. All of the trails should be seen, and the total walk is not beyond most walkers' endurance.

Among the nine acres of woods are familiar sugar maples, pitch pines, and American lindens, as well as the more rare chinquapin chestnut, cucumber magnolia, paw paw, and black haw. There is also a medicinal plant trail (see Outing 36) and an educational nature trail.

Bowman's Hill Tower stands on a hill 380 feet above sea level, one of the highest points along the Delaware River. The hill has long served as a landmark, and before Washington's crossing of the Delaware, it was used as a lookout and signal station. The present tower commands a view of 14 miles of the Delaware River Valley, including the very spot that Washington crossed. The tower can be visited and climbed every day but Tuesday year-round. There is a small admission fee.

The hike up to the tower takes you through some rather dense underbrush, but your effort is well rewarded at the top. If you prefer, you can get back in your car and drive out of the preserve, back onto Route 32, turning to the right as you exit; you will soon come to a sign to the tower. A winding drive brings you to a parking area at its base. The spectacular view from the tower is a fitting end to your walk.

After the Walk

Washington's Crossing State Park, directly across Route 32 from Bowman's Hill Preserve, is the historic site where General Washington crossed the Delaware on Christmas 1776. You can see the banks the Continental Army climbed and the houses where they rested, and you can take a tour and watch a short documentary film at Memorial Auditorium. The state park is on both sides of the Delaware River and includes all sorts of facilities, from cooking areas to picnic grounds to a Braille nature trail. This is an especially tasteful historic site, and walking through it gives a real sense of time and place. It has not been "hoked up," and we like its simplicity. Most buildings are open year-round, 9:00 A.M. to 4:30 P.M. There is a small fee for park use, but not for the historic sites.

Among the places we recommend you visit in the park are the Thompson-Neeley House, known as the House of Decision, where Washington's strategy is said to have been decided; the Point of Embarkation, with nice paths that will allow you to walk to the exact spot of the crossing; and the Old Ferry Inn (1757), which is thought to have fed the general before he set off across the river and is still furnished in the style of that time.

Lambertville, New Jersey, is New Hope's across-the-river neighbor, about 6 miles northwest on Route 32 and across the bridge. While New Hope has become a very touristy town, Lambertville prides itself on retaining a historic charm. And it is indeed a delightful place to walk and poke into, with its small old-fashioned streets and riverside spots. While wandering around, you should not miss the James Wilson Marshall House at 60 Bridge Street. A National Historic Landmark, it was the boyhood home of the man who discovered gold in California in 1848, which led to the famous gold rush. Built in 1816 in the Federal style, it is now a museum that displays pictures, maps, and artifacts showing nineteenth-century life in Lambertville. Open Saturday and Sunday from 1:00 to 4:00 P.M., or by appointment (call during the week on Tuesday, Wednesday, or Thursday.) For further information call (609) 397–0770.

If you prefer a more bustling environment, New Hope is a mecca of shops and entertainment. For a listing of things to do and see in New Hope, see Outing 38.

If you still feel energetic after your day at Bowman's Hill Preserve and want more active recreation, the Delaware River is the perfect place to be. Water sports are easily available in this area. Canoeing on the Delaware is world famous. What makes it so attractive is that the Delaware is one of the last free-flowing rivers and is portage free for 185 miles, from Hancock, New York, to Trenton, New Jersey. In addition, it is one of the last wild and scenic rivers in the East and has a great abundance of wildlife. One of the most efficiently organized places nearby where you can rent canoes or plan excursions is Point Pleasant Canoe Outfitters in Point Pleasant, Pennsylvania (a few miles north of New Hope on Route 32); call (215) 297–8823 for further information. Fishing and inner tubing are also popular on the Delaware River.

38 | A Towpath Walk along the Delaware Canal

New Hope

How to Get There: Take the New Jersey Turnpike south to exit 9, then Route 1 south toward Trenton. Pick up Interstate 95/295 south after Princeton (at Bakersville), and take the interstate to the exit at Yardley, Pennsylvania. Take Pennsylvania Route 32 west to New Hope.

The level towpath that runs alongside this picturesque Delaware Canal is an ideal walking route. Originally built to accommodate the mules that pulled barges along the canal—as they still do today—the towpath is narrow and overhung with trees; it is a scenic delight as it winds along the waterway. It is flat, and the only impediments to a solitary stroll are occasional joggers and bikers and other walkers, in addition to the mules who still ply the canal drawing barges now filled with sightseers.

If you start at its beginning, the canal walk can cover almost 60 miles, and as a matter of fact, hardy souls do just that, either taking their camping gear along or sleeping at inns along the route. Our chosen walk is quite a bit shorter, though you can lengthen it at will, particularly if you have a car parked at the other end. It is especially nice on a spring day, when the willow trees along the way are at their lightest green, and when the canal seems bright and clean.

Keep in mind as you walk that you are never very far from civilization; you can turn off the towpath now and again for refreshment at a nearby village. We preferred, however, to stay on the path, taking a picnic lunch with us.

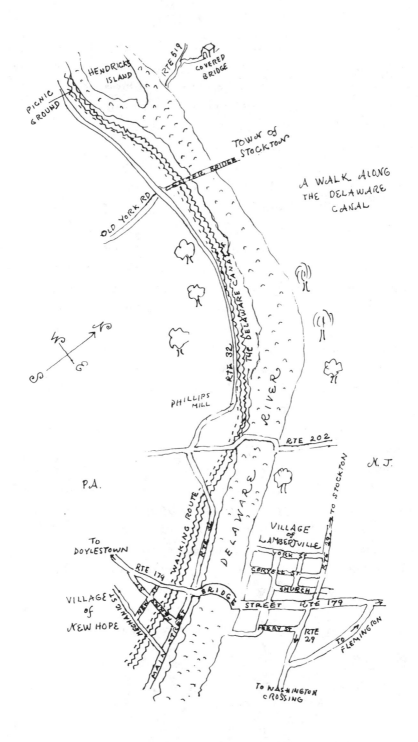

A WALK ALONG
THE DELAWARE
CANAL

HENDRICKS ISLAND

PICNIC GROUND

RTE 59

COVERED BRIDGE

TOWER of STOCKTON

OLD YORK RD

CORLETT BRIDGE

THE DELAWARE CANAL

RTE 32

PHILLIPS MILL

RIVER

RTE 202

N. J.

P.A.

WALKING ROUTE

RTE 32

DELAWARE

TO DOYLESTOWN

RTE 179

VILLAGE of NEW HOPE

MECHANICS

MAIN STREET

BRIDGE

VILLAGE of LAMBERTVILLE

RTE 202 TO STOCKTON

YORK ST

CORYELL ST

CHURCH

STREET

RTE 179

FERRY ST

RTE 29

TO FLEMINGTON

TO WASHINGTON CROSSING

N
W E
S

As we mentioned above, spring is the ideal time for this walk, although fall is also very pleasant. Summer finds New Hope such a tourist mecca that we hesitate to add more people to the crush. The towpath is always opens, so even winter walkers can use it if they enjoy the crisp waterside winds.

There are no restrictions on visitors to the towpath, or on what they take along. You can bring your dog, a picnic, and whatever else you would like to have. We suggest strong walking shoes and birding binoculars.

This canal, which is steeped in history, covers an area of Pennsylvania that is beautiful both in natural scenery and in architecture. The old stone houses for which Pennsylvania is well known sit smack along the towpath, surrounded by giant sycamores, tulip poplars, locusts, oaks, and overhanging weeping willows. Rhododendrons and hill laurel abound—another reason to go in spring. Fishermen enjoy the canal for catfish, perch, and carp, in addition to the smallmouth black bass that have traditionally been caught here. Shad, once a flourishing crop, are just beginning to make a comeback.

Birders will be well rewarded on this walk. Among the waterfowl seen at any time of year are mallard and black ducks and night herons; summertime brings egrets and ospreys. Other birds to look for are owls, downy woodpeckers, Carolina wrens, ruffed grouse, marsh hawks, ring-necked pheasants, and turkey vultures, in addition to the more common robins, cardinals, and goldfinches. In summer you might see, or at least hear, whippoor-wills. The profusion of birds along the canal is due to its proximity to the Delaware River, which serves as a guide to migratory birds—in particular Canada geese, which can sometimes be heard honking in early mornings as they wing their way along.

The Walk

Begin this section of the canal walk at New Hope, a jumble of antiques shops, historic houses, and tourist spots in a scenic location along the Delaware River. The canal goes right through New Hope, and the towpath is easily reached just east of Mechanic Street. (You might want to see lock no. 8 in New Hope before setting out.) Walk out of town along the path heading west. You will first pass the New Hope and Ivyland Railroad, which runs a steam train excursion on weekends in the tourist season. As you leave the bustle of New Hope, you will come to Rabbit Run Bridge, and then in about 1.5 miles to Phillips Mill, built as a gristmill in 1756. Once a thriving art colony, Phillips Mill is now a small community surrounding the converted mill—a nice place to take a breather. About 0.5 mile farther you can spot the remains of two old kilns where the lime industry once flourished; here lime was mixed to make mortar and crop fertilizer. About 3 miles from New Hope you'll come to Center Bridge, once known as Readings Ferry, named for Colonel John Reading, who established the first Delaware River ferry in 1711. At that time a major route from New York to Philadelphia crossed here. When you reach Center Bridge, cross over to see Stockton in New Jersey, known for its fine stone houses. There is an inn on each side of the water here. (About a mile farther on the New Jersey side you'll find Route 519, which leads to a fine covered bridge.)

The sightseeing barge stops at a picnic area surrounded by rhododendron, where there are picnic tables, grills, and a comfort station. In the center of the canal is Hendricks Island, which virtually fills up the canal. You will now have walked just under 5 miles. If you continue (assuming you have a car waiting for you), you can walk on to Lumberville, where there is another lock and nice scenery (about 2 miles along from your picnic site). From there go to Point Pleasant (2 more miles), where you'll find the remains of a river bridge and a sandy swimming beach on the Delaware. The walk continues for many miles, eventually ending at Easton, Pennsylvania, where the Lehigh River meets the Delaware.

If you prefer to begin the canal walk before New Hope, try combining a visit to Washington's Crossing and Bowman's Hill Preserve (see Outings 36 and 37) and heading west to join up with this walk at New Hope.

After the Walk

Explore New Hope and its across-the-river neighbor, Lambertville. The ferry between the two villages was built in 1726 and was known as Coryell's Ferry; you can still visit the site. Other historic reminders of the importance of this area in the Revolutionary War are all around, from Washington's Crossing, about 3 miles east, to several historic houses in New Hope. The boats used by General Washington in the crossing of the river were hidden on a small island in the Delaware near Lambertville, and the hill called Goat Mountain, just to the south of the village, was where Washington was taken to view the island to make sure the boats could not be seen. The Parry Barn Museum in New Hope (Main Street) is an eighteenth-century mansion built at the end of the Revolution and now operated by the New Hope Historical Society.

Reminders of the busy days of canal traffic also still exist: In New Hope you can take the canal-barge ride mentioned above. Contact the New Hope Barge Company at (215) 862–2842 for information on a one-hour excursion, a charming and leisurely outing, accompanied on occasion by a folksinger or tale-teller. You can also take a river sightseeing trip in a small boat from The Coryell's Ferry landing in Lambertville. For a train ride on one of the few remaining coal-burning trains around, try the excursion line mentioned above; it goes puffing along for 14 miles through scenic Bucks County, beginning in New Hope.

Those interested in historic houses and architecture might enjoy one of the various walking tours of New Hope, with its many shops. Pick up a guide at the Parry Barn Museum or any shop, or just walk along Ferry, Main, and Bridge streets.

Also worth a visit is the well-known Bucks County Playhouse, which presents professional summer stock in a 250-year-old gristmill on the water. For information call(215) 862–2041. A play can be a nice way to end a day of canal walking and exploring a bustling village.

If, however, you are still feeling energetic, you might want to try one of the many water sports that the Delaware River Valley offers. There is canoeing (this is one of the prime canoe spots in the East, and access to the canal can be gained in practically every village), inner tubing, white-water rafting, and fishing. For more information on these sports, call Point Pleasant Canoe Outfitters (215–297–8823), who can advise you when, where, and how to go about it.

39 | A Medieval-Style Stone Castle and Its Eccentric Surroundings

Grey Towers, Milford

How to Get There: From the George Washington Bridge, take Interstate 80 west to Route 15 north to Route 206 north. Continue north on Route 206 and cross the bridge over the Delaware River into Pennsylvania. Turn right to Milford and follow the signs (visit the Grey Towers Web site for details).

Few gardens that we have seen have such an esoteric architectural design as those that surround the medieval-style castle called Grey Towers. Here, in a rural, off-the-beaten-track area of eastern Pennsylvania, you'll find this castle and its one hundred acres of grounds beautifully situated on a wooded hill beyond the small town of Milford (some forty minutes from the much-traveled Interstate 80). Like the mansion, the complex garden structures, walls, patios, and pergolas, and the many outbuildings are all made of native bluestone, a picturesque and evocative material. The design of the entire estate creates a romantic sense of faraway times and places.

Grey Towers was constructed in 1886 by the Pinchot family, long residents of the area. The first Pinchot emigrated from France in 1816 (his charming house in Milford in now the Community House and public library). James Pinchot was a prosperous manufacturer; his son, Gifford, was a noted environmentalist, appointed by President Teddy Roosevelt to head the U.S. Forest Service. Gifford Pinchot became governor of Pennsylvania in 1927 and lived at Grey Towers until his death in 1946. The site was designated a National Historic Landmark (with President Kennedy in attendance) in 1963.

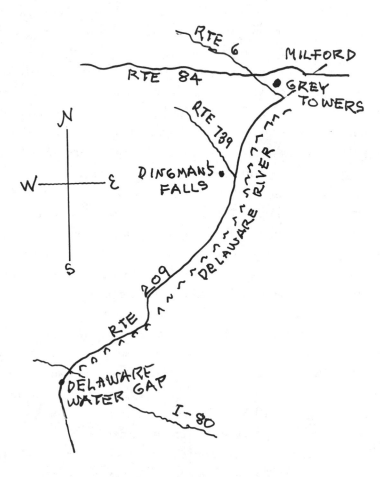

Pinchot's lifelong interest in conservation continues at Grey Towers today, where environmentalists still use the estate for conferences. For information and tours, call (570) 296–9630; www.fs.fed.us/na/gt.

The Walk

What an estate it is! The forty-one-room mansion, with its three great stone towers, is in itself a cross between French medieval design (and furnishings) and affluent nineteenth century taste. Its architect, Richard Morris Hunt (who designed the Metropolitan Museum of Art, among other grand buildings), created an American castle curiously set just outside a thoroughly ungrand village. (The house is open for public tours in summertime.)

Around the castle are many small buildings and garden areas. These constructions have such intriguing names as "The Finger Bowl," "The Bait Box," and "The Letter Box," as well as the more familiar moat, icehouse, and pergola. Pinchot's ideas for the grounds were the result of extensive travels—apparently both to foreign countries and into the past of his imagination.

Immediately beyond the dining room's French doors, for example, is "The Finger Bowl," a raised pool surrounded by a mosaic terrace and tanks for aquatic plants. The "bowl" (a unique type of water table) was created after the Pinchots returned from the South Seas Islands. Here the family occasionally dined by candlelight, sitting round its edges and eating from Polynesian serving bowls that floated in the water.

Steps lead from this terrace to another enclosed stone-walled area, once the family's swimming pool and now beautifully landscaped with wisteria vines and garden areas. The surroundings of the mansion include a complex set of gardens on different terraced levels—all of them created by the use of bluestone paths, walls, and steps, as well as ancient-seeming pergolas and trellises. Many of the surrounding terraces contain gargoyles: Turkeys and eagles, among other beasts, appear in small niches and atop marble columns. And numerous statues decorate the place, including a bust of the Marquis de Lafayette in a niche on the second story of the house.

There are vined gazebos, a rock garden, a lily pond, benches, fountains, and mosaics, plus a reflecting pool and an amphitheater (used by the family for theatricals and campaign gatherings). At the far end of the reflecting pool is "The Bait Box," built as a playhouse. Various millstones taken from local grain mills also adorn the gardens. In among these many man-made divisions and artistic ornaments are luxuriant flowers and other plantings. These are gardens in which very little of the design seems left to chance or to Mother Nature's own instincts.

All of these sites offer splendid views of the fields and wooded hillsides stretching into the distance. The trees—including a sugar maple planted by General Sherman more than a century ago—are notable. And the vast wooded sections, including a spectacular and mysterious hemlock forest, are, of course, administered by the Forest Service. This is an inviting place for a walk.

A visit to Grey Towers might suggest a central question about gardens: Can the design created by architectural elements be overwhelming? Or are flowers and other plantings at their most beautiful when organized by stone structures, rather than the boxwood hedges or groves of shrubbery favored by so many landscapists? Grey Towers is one of the most architecturally designed garden we have seen, and as such is well worth a visit to this out-of-the-way spot.

After the Walk

Visit Peters Valley, the charming crafts village in the nearby Delaware Water Gap area. Peters Valley is located on Route 615 in Layton, New Jersey, and is open year-round. Call (973) 948–5200 for information.

The Delaware Water Gap National Recreation Area south of Grey Towers is a marvelous site for hiking, boating, and picnicking. Enjoy Dingmans Falls, not far from Grey Towers. For information on activities at the Water Gap area, call (717) 588–2418.

Bird-Watching

40 | Birding, Beaching, and Hiking Off-Season on Sandy Hook

Sandy Hook, New Jersey

How to Get There: From the George Washington Bridge, take Interstate 80 west to the Garden State Parkway south. Get off at exit 117 and take New Jersey Route 36 to Atlantic Highlands. Go across the bridge to Sandy Hook. From midtown Manhattan, take the Lincoln Tunnel to the New Jersey Turnpike, to the Garden State Parkway, and follow the same directions as above.

Sandy Hook, part of the Gateway National Recreation Area, is a narrow spit of land more than 7 miles long. Its sandy beach faces the Atlantic on one side; its marshes and bay side face the mainland of the Jersey shore. Although it was developed by the New Jersey state park system as a public beach (on the ocean side), it has been left as an ecosystem of fragile marshland and tidal pools on the bay side. In between is a long roadway with occasional parking areas and a ranger station. If you visit Sandy Hook at a non-swimming time, you'll be amazed by the size of the area that has been left in its natural state. Off-season or on a rainy day you're not apt to meet many people hiking on either length of the Hook.

The ocean side of Sandy Hook has a wide beach with nice rolling breakers and the usual miscellaneous Atlantic flotsam, particularly out of season. A walk beginning at the first parking lot, either along the sand (hard walking except close by the waterline) and/or on the top section of the flat rock breakwater at beach's edge, can take you 7 miles.

If you are a birder, you will prefer the other side of this narrow spit of land, for once you make your way to the bay side, you'll be on a small shell-covered beach that winds in and out of the bay inlets, depending on the tides. Birds are everywhere. Hundreds of gulls and other seabirds live along this coast, making raucous noise and generally enjoying the carefully preserved ecosystem. The marshlands are mostly closed to the public, but if you take your binoculars, you can see all kinds of birds swooping in and out of the dune grass and waterfront.

Sand spits like Sandy Hook are buffeted by winds and waves. The vegetation that grows on barrier beaches like this is diverse; beach plum, prickly pear cactus, dusty miller—and large amounts of poison ivy—are indigenous. Also growing here is a holly forest (that can only be seen on special tours given by the park system), an oddity that is part of the closed environment. Some of the holly trees are thought to be more than 300 years old, and their red berries keep many birds wintering here. Both prickly pear and beach heather also proliferate, despite the harsh sandy soil.

Out of season you'll find Sandy Hook an especially fine place to enjoy the Atlantic coastline. In clear weather you can see the buildings of New York City, and yet you're in such a wonderful, natural spot!

The terrain is as unhilly as a sand flat and is ideal for any walker. Kids will enjoy beachcombing the waterfront (on both sides) and the great windy openness of the area. Take your own food and drink, your binoculars, a good windbreaker, and shoes that can get sandy or wet.

The park is open year-round. Summer is not recommended for walkers or birders—except on rainy days—because beach traffic is so heavy at this most northern of New Jersey's shorefronts. During the season there is a parking fee; off-season there is no charge and absolutely no congestion. The only visitors you

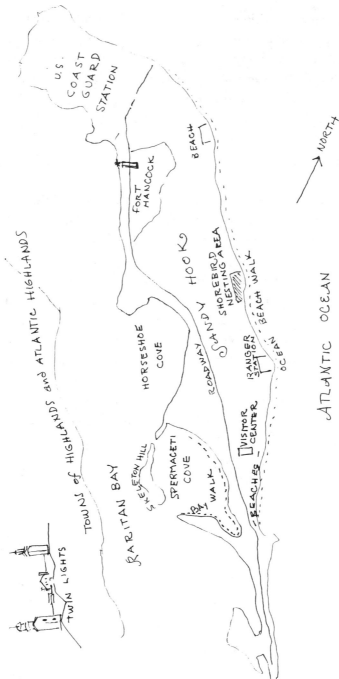

U.S. COAST GUARD STATION

BEACH

FORT HANCOCK

SANDY HOOK

SHOREBIRD NESTING AREA

BEACH WALK

HORSESHOE COVE

ROADWAY

RANGER STATION

OCEAN

VISITOR CENTER

SKELETON HILL

SPERMACETI COVE

BEACHES

BAY WALK

RARITAN BAY

TOWNS of HIGHLANDS and ATLANTIC HIGHLANDS

TWIN LIGHTS

ATLANTIC OCEAN

NORTH

are likely to encounter are fishermen. Sandy Hook has good birding and hiking whenever you go. In fall you'll see waterfowl and shorebirds heading south, the marsh shrubs turning color, and great sunsets. In winter you'll enjoy beachcombing on the ocean side, and spotting ducks, herring and black-backed gulls, as well as an occasional kittiwake or gannet. Spring visitors, particularly early in the morning, will see shorebirds in breeding plumage, warblers, hawks, kestrels, and even peregrine falcons in migrating season. Songbird and raptor flights are common in April and May.

Remember that an ocean wind is a cold wind, so bundle up if you come in winter or early spring.

The Walk

There are several ways to explore Sandy Hook. We suggest you begin by driving to the information station first, to pick up a map of the various sections. The beach and bay walk (best for birders) is around Spermaceti Cove (named for a beached whale long ago). To take this walk, park at Lot C, cross the road, and go down to the bay side. Birds you should look for here include some 267 species, of which 49 are considered unusual. Rare or endangered birds include the grebe, gannet, Wilson's phalarope, Hudsonian godwit, osprey (which nests on Sandy Hook), black rail, roseate tern, and white-rumped sandpiper, among others. Breeding birds include the clapper rail, great horned owl, whip-poor-will, common flicker, barn swallow, robin, towhee, fish crow, and brown thrasher. Gulls and other common waterbirds are everywhere.

Other seasonal wildlife to look for include horseshoe crabs in warm weather, which arrive on the beach to spawn; monarch butterflies, which come in droves to feed on the fall goldenrod on their way to wintering in Mexico; brant (small geese), which winter close to the bay shoreline; and some 50,000 broadbills (scaup), which drift and feed in rafts.

There is a shorebird nesting colony on the ocean side some 2 miles north of Spermaceti Cove. Those walking along the ocean will be able to spot more birds there. The Old Dune Trail, which begins near the visitor center, will take you through a birdviewing area also. Guided tours of ecological interest are also available. Inquire at the visitor center, or call (732) 872–5970.

If you prefer ocean beach walking to birding, try parking your car at Area D and setting off away from civilization. You'll find even fewer people and less trammeled beach. Look along the beach for flotsam, or simply enjoy the incoming waves and changing color of the ocean. Of course, if you can arrange to have a car waiting for you at the far end of your walk, you can go on for miles and miles.

After the Walk

At the farther end of Sandy Hook is Fort Hancock, which has both a lighthouse and museum. But we found the most interesting nearby attraction to be Twin Lights. If you look back toward shore from the beginning of Sandy Hook, you'll see two rather ancient-looking lighthouses high on the hill. Twin Lights was constructed in 1828 as the Navesink Light Station. The towers, which are not identical, are some 256 feet above sea level. If your legs are still agile after your walk, you can climb the towers (about sixty-five steps) and get a great view. If you don't want to climb, you can still enjoy a nice display at Twin Lights, which we recommend. Here, one of the first wireless transmissions in America went out, when Marconi telegraphed reports in 1899 of the America's Cup race off Sandy Hook. There are also exhibits about lighthouse lenses, shore boats, and other nautical subjects concerning this once very dangerous coastal area. To get to Twin Lights, retrace your route to the town of Atlantic Highlands and make your way up the winding roads to the top of the hill.

41 | Birding in a New Jersey Highland

Scherman-Hoffman Wildlife Sanctuary, Bernardsville, New Jersey

How to Get There: From the George Washington Bridge, take Interstate 80 west to Interstate 287 south. Exit I-287 at Bernardsville, go west, past the intersection with Route 202, and proceed on Child's Road to Hardscrabble Road (turn right). Continue up the hill to the Hoffman Center; go left a short distance to the Scherman Center. These twin centers' trails intersect, but you can start from either place.

These 240 acres of rolling countryside, dogwood trees, and waving grass are a particularly nice birding spot. Administered by the Audubon Society with a minimum of signs or intrusions, the sanctuary provides a series of hillside trails through wood and field and along streams that are a delight to birder and stroller alike.

The Hoffman section at the top of the hill provides a typically highland environment for native birds, while the adjoining Scherman section includes the lower-lying riverside habitat, so a visit here can give you a chance to spot a great variety of birds. In fact, more than 125 species have been sighted at this location. Both land birds and waterbirds are familiar in the sanctuary. In addition, the centers offer a variety of programs dealing with birding, as well as guided field trips in rainy or sunny weather. For those with other naturalistic interests, the centers feature tree and lichen identification workshops and a variety of other programs.

This site is one of many sanctuaries and nature centers that the New Jersey Audubon Society (908–204–8998) administers. In each of these, a different variety of habitat means different sorts of birding, as well as diverse kinds of strolling. This walk is some-what hilly for elderly walkers, but very nice for families with energetic kids. The rough state of the pathways through the woods and the rolling terrain make this a slightly strenuous walk, but you can go slowly, of course. Wear boots or wet-shoes (par-ticularly in spring), and take binoculars and your lunch for a wonderful day's outing. The centers are open from 9:00 A.M. to 5:00 P.M. Tuesday through Saturday, and noon to 5:00 P.M. on Sunday. Telephone: 908-204-8998.

For a list of events, programs, and daily sightings, call (908) 766–5787.

The Walk

Leave your car at either of the two centers, depending on whether you prefer the riverside or the more hilly woods. A trail map is available at both spots. Among the birds to look for are migrating land birds in the spring, including robins, bluebirds, and many types of warblers; in fall you'll spot dark-eyed juncos, tufted titmice, chickadees, white-throated sparrows, cardinals, and (circling overhead) turkey vultures and red-tailed hawks. Down at the water's edge you might find wood ducks, great blue herons, and kingfishers. This is an excellent spot to visit in springtime when the dogwoods are in bloom and the migrant birds are arriving.

42 | Bird-Watching in the Great Swamp

Morris and Somerset Counties, New Jersey

How to Get There: From the George Washington Bridge, take Interstate 80 west to Interstate 287 south. Get off at exit 26A and follow the signs for the Great Swamp National Wildlife Refuge.

The Great Swamp National Wildlife Refuge—a vast (over 6,000 acres) area of swamp woodland, hardwood ridges, marsh, grassland, brush, ponds, and pastureland only 26 miles west of New York City—is a rare environment in which to view birds and other wildlife. This rich land was destined to become the site of an airport in the late 1950s. Fortunately, a band of local citizens and others joined forces, raised funds, and donated the bulk of the swamp property to the U.S. Department of the Interior to guarantee that it would remain forever wild.

Since the late 1960s the swamp has been designated as a wilderness area, a refuge for more than 200 species of birds, as well as for a surprisingly large variety of mammals, reptiles, and amphibians. The fact that it is a "wilderness area" means that motorized traffic is forbidden in certain sections and severely restricted in others, making parking limited and access somewhat difficult. It also means that only the more determined birders and nature watchers roam through the fairly remote trails in this vast terrain, experiencing a true wilderness habitat with its rich variety of migratory birds and other animals. You can, however, also drive through the refuge or walk on marked trails.

There are two different ways to go birding in the Great Swamp. Within the swamp there is a Wildlife Observation Center off Long Hill Road. Here you can observe and photograph birds and other animals from blinds set in the surrounding boardwalk trails. Organized tours are occasionally provided for those who prefer going in a group. This center is within a wildlife management area where research studies are conducted; grasslands and brush are occasionally cut back to ensure the best habitat for the diversity of species, and nesting environments are provided for ducks and other birds.

On the western edge of the Great Swamp is the much smaller Lord Stirling Park with its Environmental Education Center. Here bird- and nature-watching are a somewhat easier proposition, as the center provides a large parking facility and easily accessible trails that start right there. Included in the park are some 8 miles of marked walking trails, as well as a boardwalk especially designed for the physically challenged and young children.

The center provides a wide variety of year-round seasonal activities for people of all ages. For example, in winter it features search parties (to find out where insects go), discussions on hibernation, exploration of the terrain on snowshoes, nature photography workshops, film and slide shows, owl prowls, marsh meanders, moonlight cross-country skiing, and maple sugaring. Throughout the year the center posts a wildlife sighting list in its headquarters, which indicates what animals and birds have been spotted recently and where they can be seen.

Walking the Great Swamp trails (including Lord Stirling Park) is fairly easy because the land is generally flat. Anyone who is interested in nature and the environment, particularly in birds, will enjoy this special habitat. It's a fine place for a visit any time of the year, bearing in mind that migratory birds are best seen in spring and fall. In spring, summer, and early fall you will see masses of wildflowers throughout. Some 200 species of flowering plants are found here and are listed in a free booklet available at the center.

As most birders know, for the most successful birding you should plan on arriving early in the morning or late in the afternoon. Bring along waterproof gear or sturdy shoes that can get wet. During the summer months it might be a good idea to bring insect repellent to ward off mosquitoes, ticks, and deer flies.

For further information contact the refuge manager at (973) 425–1222.

The Walk

The easier walk begins at the Environmental Center, where you can leave your car. Inside the headquarters you can get a number of free fliers that describe the variety of animal and plant life, as well as a list of current sightings. Among the birds you can expect to see (depending on the season) are the mallard and black duck, green heron, Canada goose, green-winged and blue-winged heron, hawk, sora, common snipe, yellow-billed and black-billed cuckoo, indigo bunting, blue-winged warbler, mourning dove, eastern screech owl, red-winged blackbird, and various types of woodpecker, to name a few. If you're lucky, you might see the blue-spotted salamander, a rare species found only here in all of New Jersey. There are many mammals in the region, including shrews, voles, beavers, occasional foxes, river otters, and long-tailed weasels. Some bear tracks were recently spotted, though bears are rarely observed in the refuge. The most common mammal to be found is the white-tailed deer, of which there are an estimated several hundred in number at the present time.

There are basically two marked trails within Lord Stirling Park, as well as the relatively short boardwalk described above. These trails begin near the headquarters and continue past the pretty pond area and into the woods. They are both loops, so you don't have to retrace your steps.

If you prefer walking through the heart of the Great Swamp, we suggest you first drive to the refuge headquarters maintenance complex on Plains Road, past the south gate, a rather hostile-looking entrance with road spikes on one side to prevent people from exiting with their cars there. You can get information concerning where best to leave your car and start off from there. You can also pick up a map of the wilderness trail system, as distinct from the more accessible and less forbidding Lord Stirling section. Remember not to park or stop your car except in designated spots within the refuge. The eastern section encompasses the wilderness area with its 8.5 miles of hiking trails. Parking space (with room for only a few cars) is found on the outer reaches of this area.

Other Birding Locations Nearby

Other sites in New Jersey offer different varieties of birds. The Lorrimer Sanctuary at 790 Ewing Avenue in Franklin Lakes (about thirty-five minutes from the city) attracts lakeside birds. Call (201) 891–2185 for information. One of the newest New Jersey birding sites is the Plainsboro Preserve in Cranbury. Among the species to spot are herons, great egrets, and other waterbirds. Phone (609) 897–9400 for more details.

43 | Bird-Watching in a Shady Conifer Forest

Muttontown Nature Preserve, Long Island

How to Get There: From midtown Manhattan, take the Midtown Tunnel to the Long Island Expressway to exit 41 north. Take Route 106 north to its intersection with Route 25A , and go left (west) a very short distance. When you reach the Howard Johnson (on your right), cross the highway to Muttontown Lane, which will take you right to the entrance.

Muttontown Nature Preserve consists of 550 acres of woodlands, fields, marshes, and a conifer stand, all prettily nestled on Long Island's North Shore. It's a spot we recommend for birders—because of its variety of terrain, many different species of birds can be seen here all year. The preserve includes lands that were once country estates or farms, but are now being allowed to return to their natural state. It also includes mature woodlands that have been in existence for generations. With its pleasantly winding (but mostly flat) trails through wooded land and field, it is an oasis of peace and quiet where the sounds you hear are those of its birds or the breeze through grassy fields or forests. Some of the trails were once bridle paths from the days when the region was dotted with elegant horse farms. (There are still quite a few; in fact, the visitor is likely to meet an occasional rider, as there are equestrian trails within the confines of the preserve.)

The birder or nature watcher has the choice of several well-marked trails, all of which are explained in maps and informative pamphlets on the birds, trees, wildflowers, mammals, reptiles, and amphibians that may be found at particular times of the year. These free materials are available at the nature center.

As in all bird-watching, the best time to view birds is early in the morning or late in the day. Spring and fall—with their migrations—bring the greatest numbers, but there is plenty to see in summer and winter, too. In fact, winter is a fine time, as you can spot birds more easily without their being camouflaged by the foliage.

This is a surprisingly cool spot, recommended for hot days, for the great trees make it shady, and it is close enough to the water to pick up ocean breezes. The walk is fairly easy, one that anyone can do. Take your usual birding gear. Remember not to collect plants, minerals, or animals; build fires; litter; or wander off trails.

The preserve is open daily from 9:30 A.M. to 4:30 P.M. For further information call (516) 571–8500.

The Walk

After you have left your car at the parking area outside the nature center, enter the small building to gather whatever information interests you. We recommend you pick up a map of the preserve. There are also several separate brochures listing birds to be found during each season, as well as material on other animals and plants to identify.

The paths meander through several ecological environments, each of which is home to different species of plants and animals. Follow blue or green blazes through the moist woodsy swamplands, where red maples, pin oaks, and ferns proliferate. Here you will see warblers during spring and fall. In the fields you will find many wildflowers, as well as vines, shrubs, and tall grasses. Bobwhites and pheasants thrive in this habitat. The woodland area of relatively young trees—forty or fifty years old—has many white ash, dogwood, apple, red maple, black cherry, and white pine. In the particularly quiet and peaceful conifer stand, where eastern white pine and European larch were planted in the early part of the twentieth century, you might spot chickadees, kinglets, crossbills, and pine siskins, among others. The rolling hills, with their small ponds surrounded by persimmon trees, attract populations of aquatic insects, amphibians, and reptiles. Finally, the mature woodlands of black oak, chestnut oak, black birch, and Norway spruce of mixed ages are the perfect habitat for many different birds, including woodpeckers, hawks, and owls. You can choose where you want to go, depending on what you wish to see.

In springtime you might see the Canada goose, snow goose, mallard, mourning dove, crow, black-capped chickadee, robin, red-winged blackbird, grackle, starling, tree sparrow, and dark-eyed junco. Sometimes, though rarely, you might see the turkey vulture, merlin, peregrine falcon, purple martin, fish crow, winter wren, gray-cheeked thrush, vesper sparrow, or bobolink.

In summer you will likely find bobwhites, ring-necked pheasants, blue jays, black-capped chickadees, catbirds, blue-winged warblers, yellowthroats, red-winged blackbirds, grackles, house finches, goldfinches, and chipping sparrows. On rare occasions you might spot the peregrine falcon, black-backed gull, Blackburnian warbler, or great egret.

In autumn you may see the American robin, cedar waxwing, parula warbler, American crow, black–capped chickadee, song sparrow, starling, or Blackburnian warbler, among the many varieties that appear at that time. Less likely are the snipe, ring-billed gull, cowbird, yellow-throated vireo, and great black-backed gull, though some have been spotted in the past.

Finally, in winter look for the Canada goose, bobwhite, ring-necked pheasant, herring gull, mourning dove, blue jay, robin, starling, cardinal, evening grosbeak, tree sparrow, and song sparrow. If you're lucky, you may even see rough-legged hawks, woodcocks, belted kingfishers, or white-winged crossbills.

Follow the well-marked trails, use your guides, and enjoy the birds!

After the Walk

You are near several major North Shore attractions: Visit the Vanderbilt Mansion (see Outing 14) or the home and grounds of Teddy Roosevelt's Sagamore Hill (Outing 16); or drive out to the beach and breakwater at Eatons Neck (Outing 17).

On your way home, you can stop at Udall's Cove, a recent addition to Long Island's preserves. It is near Little Neck, between Northern Boulevard, and 243rd and 247th Streets. Here, fifty acres of wetlands and woodlands provide a wonderful habitat for migratory egrets, herons, ibises, peregrine falcons, and some 300 other species to delight bird-watchers.

44 | Birding in Jamaica Bay Wildlife Refuge
Queens, New York

How to Get There: By subway, take the IND line (A train) to Broad Channel, then walk west to Cross Bay Boulevard and north 0.75 mile. By car, take the Midtown Tunnel to the Long Island Expressway to Woodhaven Boulevard, which becomes Cross Bay Boulevard, which will go right into the area. Park at the headquarters, where you can also pick up information on the layout of the refuge.

Although this wonderful birding spot is technically in New York City, its astonishing array of birds makes it hard to believe its so-called urban location. It is directly across the bay from the John F. Kennedy Airport, and in clear weather you can actually see the skyscrapers of Manhattan. But more than 250 species of birds are found here, including rare and uncommon ones. So, even though we have not included other city locations, we couldn't leave out Jamaica Bay for our birders and other walkers seeking interesting terrain.

Jamaica Bay Wildlife Refuge, part of the Gateway National Recreation Area, was formerly Jamaica Bay Park, a city park planted deliberately to suit the tastes of birds by a man named Herbert Johnson. Now it is administered by the federal government and is one of the most beloved birders' sites on the East Coast. Storm damage to trees and other plants is carefully repaired. The administration provides a lecture room, restrooms, and an information desk. No refreshments are available, no picnicking allowed, and, of course, no collecting or disturbing the habitat.

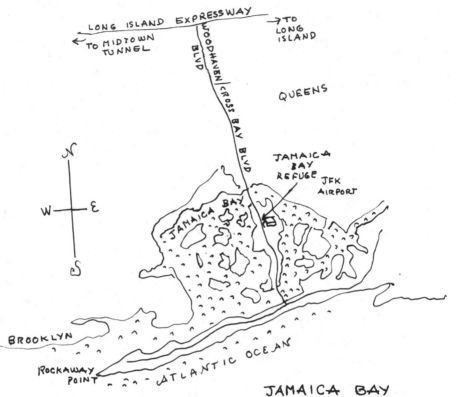

JAMAICA BAY
WILDLIFE REFUGE

You can get more information on Jamaica Bay and its possibilities by writing to the Jamaica Bay Unit of the Gateway National
Recreation Area, Floyd Bennett Field, Brooklyn, NY 11234, or by
calling the New York Audubon Society at (212) 691–7483, which
can tell you what birds to look for at different times.

This extraordinary and unusual terrain includes a shrubby
woodland, a grassy area called the north garden, and a large area
of marshes, a beach area (occasionally closed when birds are
nesting), a freshwater pond, and many walks with observation
points. This is a fine place for a full day's walking and observing. The birds seen here include more than fifty varieties,

among them the glossy ibis, greater scaup, hooded merganser, osprey, white-rumped sandpiper, roseate tern, summer tanager, Lapland longspur, European widgeon, and some rare warblers. You are more likely to spot egrets, ruddy ducks, white-crowned sparrows, and snow geese, as well as robins, hermit thrushes, and Cape May warblers.

Fall and spring migratory birds are everywhere in Jamaica Bay, making it an excellent outing for birders. Rare winter birds include the peregrine falcon, the black-headed gull, and many seabirds.

45 | Birding in Rural Westchester

Ward Pound Ridge Reservation, Cross River, New York

How to Get There: From uptown Manhattan, take the Major Deegan Expressway, which becomes the New York State Thruway, to the Cross County Parkway, to the Hutchinson River Parkway, to Interstate 684 north to Route 35 (turn right). Stay on Route 35 until you come to the junction of Route 121, and follow the signs to the reservation.

The Ward Pound Ridge Reservation is an ideal birding and hiking area for those seeking to combine a natural environment and bird habitat. This vast reservation—some 5,000 acres of woodland, open fields, swampland, ravines, and a hidden pond—is home or breeding ground to more than a hundred species. It is situated within rural Westchester County on the border of Connecticut in a region of rolling hills, old stone walls, rustic homesteads, and wonderful country air. Even if you are not a birder, we recommend this peaceful sanctuary for its 35 miles of scenic walking trails (including four self-guided trails) that provide a real respite from urban life. As you wander about you may cross paths with an occasional horseback rider—this is horse country—perhaps a cross-country skier or two on a crisp winter day, or another walker on a nature outing. The park is spacious and never feels crowded within its many winding trails, even on busy weekends.

The reservation has additional facilities that make it a good place for families with children. The Trailside Nature Museum, with its specimens of birds, mammals, reptiles, insects, and minerals, as well as its well-regarded Delaware Indian Resource Center, is a good place to browse before or after your walk.

Here you can also pick up information about the park: a map showing the trails, a calendar of park events, and a list of birds that have recently been sighted. The museum is open Tuesday, Wednesday, Thursday, and Saturday from 9:00 A.M. to 4:00 P.M. Call (914) 864–7322 for details.

There are over two dozen rustic stone and wooden shelters for campers, some picnicking facilities, areas for sledding (far enough away from trails so as not to disturb birders and others seeking peace and quiet), and a charming half-acre wildflower garden with a hundred labeled varieties.

An outing to Ward Pound Ridge is recommended at any time of year, because of the birds that come here, even in winter. The terrain varies from somewhat hilly to fairly flat; it is not difficult for the average walker. There are restrictions: no hunting, no fires (except in designated areas), no unleashed pets, no collecting either minerals or plants, no capturing animals or trapping. Fishing is allowed in certain areas. The reservation is open all year from 9:00 A.M. to 5:00 P.M. For information call (914) 763–3493.

The Walk

Leave your car (for a small fee, in season) in one of the designated areas; parking is not allowed along roadsides. If you're here on a day when the museum is open, go there first to pick up a map or a list of birds. Otherwise, you can get park information at the main office near the entrance.

The trails you choose and where you set off will depend in part on the types of habitats that interest you. Wetlands, hills, ponds, and rocky areas are marked on the map. In the wetlands—profuse with mosses, marsh marigolds, skunk cabbage, and blueberry bushes—you will see ducks and other waterfowl, as well as frogs and salamanders. Look for bluebirds near the large maple trees.

Other birds (depending on the season) include the Canada goose, northern harrier, sharp-shinned hawk, red-tailed hawk, ruffed grouse, rock dove, mourning dove, downy woodpecker, hairy woodpecker, northern flicker, horned lark, purple martin, cliff swallow, black-capped chickadee, tufted titmouse, golden-crowned kinglet, gray catbird, northern mockingbird, brown thrasher, cedar waxwing, European starling, blue-winged warbler, Tennessee warbler, Blackburnian warbler, ovenbird, common yellowthroat, rose-breasted grosbeak, song sparrow, swamp sparrow, common grackle, northern oriole, and house finch. Of course, many birds are spotted only occasionally or rarely. Among the rare species that have been seen here are the American bittern, American black duck, bald eagle, merlin, upland sandpiper, long-eared owl, northern saw-whet owl, olive-sided flycatcher, northern shrike, marsh wren, pine warbler, clay-colored sparrow, red crossbill, white-winged crossbill, and common redpoll.

Other Birding Locations Nearby

There are several other bird-watching spots in Westchester, not far from the city, that bear mentioning. Among them are two that are administered by the Saw Mill River Audubon Society; both are in Chappaqua.

The Gedney Brook Sanctuary consists of some sixty acres of swampland, ridge, and rocky landscape. This preserve is particularly noted for its woodpeckers, but there are many other varieties to be seen. Since there is much wet and marshy land in this sanctuary, you'll find quite a few waterbirds, including wood ducks, mallards, and spotted sandpipers.

The other preserve, quite nearby, is the Pinecliff Sanctuary. This one also has a special conservation aim: preserving wetlands and the species of wildlife that enjoy them. This is a small sanctuary of just about seven acres, but you'll find a wide variety of pond life to watch, including toads, frogs, salamanders, and dragonflies. Birds spotted here include crested flycatchers in spring.

46 | Birding in the Marshland Conservancy
Rye, New York

N

w——*E*

S

How to Get There: From the George Washington Bridge, take the Cross Bronx Expressway to the Bruckner Expressway, to Interstate 95, to exit 18B (Mamaroneck Avenue); bear right and take a left onto Route 1. The entrance to the conservancy is on your right.

The Marshland Conservancy is a nice spot for birding and walking in close proximity to the city. Surrounded by elegant and imposing mansions with columned facades, it once was the private estate of John Jay, the first chief justice of the United States, and is now a preserve owned and operated by the County of Westchester. This rural tract of land includes a great variety of habitats—woodlands, marshes, mudflats, and a nice big field—that provide a haven for all kinds of birds and other animals. It is an appealing, scenic spot, where you can walk through the quiet woods, view seashore marshes with tall grasses from a panoramic lookout, or meander across the vast, open field. The preserve is refreshing in its simplicity: There are few signs of organized activity, few dos and don'ts. It's simply a place for quiet observation, where you can watch birds and other animals unhampered by outside interruptions.

There is a small, discreet museum with exhibits of local plants and animals, as well as a couple of pleasing trails that circle through the woods and fields, where you might spot an occasional pheasant or even a great horned owl. This is a good place to visit throughout the year, as there is always something of interest. The field, which was once a wheat field and is now left alone with only occasional tending, is filled with varieties of wildflowers.

In summer it is ablaze with orange butterfly weed; in early fall, it becomes a mass of yellow, with its profusion of goldenrod and sunflowers.

The Walk

Leave your car at the small parking area next to the shelter. You have a choice of a couple of interconnecting trails that wander through the woods, alongside and into the fields, eventually leading you to the overlook with its dramatic view onto the marshes and Milton Harbor below. You can continue your walk, going down to the marsh, on the beach alongside the bay, and out to a narrow stretch called Marie's Neck, for another scenic panoramic view. (Watch out for poison ivy!)

This rich habitat attracts all kinds of animals. The marsh grasses provide food for crabs, mussels, clams, snails, and other animals that in turn attract such birds as snowy and great egrets, great blue herons, and both black- and yellow-crowned herons. In fact, this is considered one of the best places on the nearby shore to view these varieties of wildlife. Along the seashore you can expect to see many different kinds of ducks, as well as herring, great black-backed, and ring-billed gulls. Along the beach look for horseshoe crabs, particularly in late May and early June, when they lay their eggs. If you're lucky, you might spot the rare wood sandpiper, sighted here recently for the first time since visiting the continent in 1907.

47 | Rambling and Birding in Connecticut

Audubon Center, Greenwich; Larsen Sanctuary, Fairfield; and Devil's Den, Weston

How to Get There: The Audubon Center in Greenwich is located at 613 Riversville Road, Greenwich, but it is nearer to Armonk, New York, than downtown Greenwich. From midtown Manhattan, take the Henry Hudson Parkway (West Side Highway) or Major Deegan Expressway to the Cross County Parkway, to the Hutchinson River Parkway, which runs into the Merritt Parkway. Take exit 28 and go north for 1.4 miles to John Street. Riversville Road is 1.4 miles farther. For Larsen Sanctuary, follow the above directions to the Merritt Parkway, take exit 44, and turn right immediately at the bottom of the ramp, onto Congress Street. At the first traffic light, take a right onto Burr Street. The center is about 1 mile down the road, on the left. For Devil's Den in Weston, follow the above directions to the Merritt Parkway, take exit 42, and go north on Route 57 for 5 miles. Turn right on Godfrey Road and then left on Pent Road.

The following three birding areas are all in nearby Connecticut. Each has a slightly different ambiance, but all are especially nice outings for just plain walkers, as well as for bird-watchers. Of course, migrating season (spring and fall) is best for seeing birds. However, we recommend these walks year-round (except on slippery ice or snow) because the scenery of each will give you a fine taste of Connecticut countryside, with its hidden ponds and lakes, tall trees, giant boulders, and old stone walls. While there are many other sanctuaries in the western part of the state, we think these three are among the nicest.

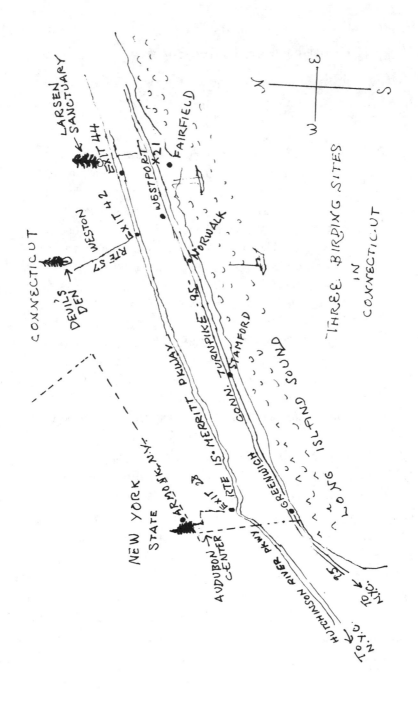

THREE BIRDING SITES IN CONNECTICUT

You can telephone the numbers given below to find out what birds are being spotted at any given time. A checklist is also available at the Audubon headquarters at the Greenwich and Fairfield sites. Though experts tell us that birds are fewer in Connecticut than they used to be, there are still plenty to be sighted. Take your binoculars and your walking shoes! But leave dogs (even leashed) at home.

The Walks

Audubon Center in Greenwich

These woodsy 477 acres have both rocky forest paths and a hidden lake (Lake Mead) deep within the preserve. The quiet of the countryside is broken only by birdcalls; when we were there it was very uncrowded, and the pristine stillness was perfect for bird-watching. About 190 species have been seen here, 87 of them nesting. There are field, thicket, lake, swamp, stream, and orchard habitats, as well as a self-guiding trail. Remains of stone walls from earlier farming days—for which New England is so well known—add to the interest of the walk, and there are varieties of indigenous trees, mushrooms, wildflowers, turtles, frogs, and other wildlife.

The forest walk was very pretty in the autumn, with the sun filtering through bright tree leaves, but it was the lake and its rocky path and dam to walk across that were particularly striking. The colors of the foliage reflected on the water made a striking background for viewing birds as they came to dip in the lake. There are two wonderful bird blinds on the edges of the lake; tall wooden towers with rustic seats and lookout space allowed us to prop binoculars on the sill and stare silently and unseen at the still water and the swooping birds.

Different seasons, of course, bring different birds. Among the nesting species to be found here are the green heron, Canada goose, ruby-throated hummingbird, four kinds of woodpeckers, and fourteen kinds of warblers. In fact, warblers seen here include some of the most uncommon species found in the Northeast. Cedar waxwings, flycatchers, vireos, and (rarely) the eastern bluebird and Philadelphia vireo have been sighted. The center recommends May for best birding (warblers especially), but other seasons are also rewarding. In October there is a hawk watch, as well as various other specific events for birders: natural history walks, trail hikes, watches for particular birds, and ecology workshops. A trail guide booklet is available that describes each habitat, includes a map, and also provides a checklist of birds.

The walk in this Audubon Center is rather hilly, but the footing is clearly marked and easy, over soft pine-needled paths. We do not recommend it for those who dislike a bit of a climb, though some of the paths are on a grassy knoll at the top. But if you have enough stamina not to puff going up a hill or two, it's a pleasant place for a birder's outing. Open daily from 9:00 A.M. to 5:00 P.M. For further information call (203) 869–5272.

Larsen Sanctuary in Fairfield

This 170-acre preserve is another Audubon sanctuary. The center located here is surrounded by 6.5 miles of trails in a gentle wilderness area. There is a woodchip-lined path that takes the walker through forest, ponds, and swampland. Particularly resplendent in autumn when the maples and other trees are at their brilliant best, this sanctuary reminds us of what Connecticut must have looked like before the villages and suburbs grew up.

Among the many birds sighted here are woodpeckers, whose workmanship can be spotted, barn and tree swallows, mourning doves, American goldfinches, and ruby-throated humming-birds. Other visitors to the area include cedar waxwings, migrating warblers, nuthatches, mockingbirds, belted kingfishers, kinglets, grosbeaks, swamp sparrows, and starlings. The center gives out a complete list for checking and will tell you what to look for at any particular time.

Among the most interesting features of this walk are the wood duck boxes sitting on poles in the middle of the pond. These boxes allow wood ducks to nest, and birders can be well rewarded at seeing them. The best seasons for visiting Larsen Sanctuary are, of course, migrating time (spring and fall); but it is open year-round, and the visitor will find birds of interest at any time.

The center has an added attraction for the blind and physically challenged. A "singing and fragrance walk" begins near the parking area. This is a smooth path with a wooden railing that allows visitors to move through heavily scented bushes and flowers and listen to various birdcalls. Since much of birding involves listening rather than seeing, this trail seems like a wonderful idea, and the center has done a good job with it.

The Larsen Sanctuary is open from 9:00 A.M. to 4:30 P.M. Tuesday through Saturday and noon to 4:30 P.M. on Sunday. The grounds are open all the time, year-round.

Devil's Den in the Lucius Pond Ordway Preserve, Weston

This is one of the prettiest walks we have taken. The sight of the lake, when we came upon it, hidden away in the woods, with the trees reflected brilliantly on the still surface, brought to mind impressionist paintings. The natural hilliness of the landscape, the bits of old stone walls and fallen tree limbs, and the rushing water over the dam where colonial millers once worked were all especially appealing. And, in addition, there are birds! Instead of the carefully arranged habitats in so many nature preserves, we found Devil's Den wonderfully underdeveloped. (Though there are a few signs giving details about an old charcoal oven and the dam.)

Devil's Den gets its name from hoofprint-shaped marks that were found on some of the rocks. Turn-of-the-century charcoal makers believed these prints were made by the devil's hot feet! We saw neither the marks nor the devil, but we did spot a variety of interesting trees, birds, frogs, and other wildlife. Devil's Den includes 1,540 acres, with approximately 20 miles of trails. A map is obtainable at the entrance from a small wooden box, where you can also sign in. There is great variety in this large area, and the map will help you choose among woods, pond, swamp, and the beautiful lakeside trail.

The lake draws a wide variety of waterfowl, including the heron, Canada goose, mallard duck, and osprey. Among the other birds sighted at Devil's Den are the sharp-shinned hawk, ruffed grouse, woodcock, mourning dove, chimney swift, slate-colored junco, belted kingfisher, scarlet tanager, several kinds of woodpecker, and the familiar jays, crows, chickadees, and robins. Rarer visitors are the thrush, red-winged blackbird, towhee, swamp sparrow, yellow-billed cuckoo, and the great horned owl.

Walking around Devil's Den is fairly easy. The trails we took were well marked, soft underfoot, and carefully constructed over obstacles. In fact, plank bridges across streams and small gorges are covered with chicken wire to keep walkers from slipping. The many large boulders of the Connecticut landscape provide nice resting spots, particularly on the banks of the lake.

There is no fee, and the preserve is open from dawn to dusk. Devil's Den suggests telephoning (203–226–4991) for a permit, but you may register on the day of your hike. We arrived and walked through without ever spotting another soul, including anyone to issue us a permit. Devil's Den belongs to the Nature Conservancy, a national nonprofit environmental organization that has been in existence since 1951.

Choosing an Outing

An Interest in Art

Aldrich Museum of Contemporary Art, Connecticut | 35
Caramoor, New York (estate and museum) | 20
Georgian Court College, New Jersey | 05
Heckscher Art Museum, Long Island | 13
Edward Hopper House, New York (gallery and historic home) | 31
Hudson River artists' sites, New York | 25
Donald M. Kendall Sculpture Garden, New York | 20
Litchfield Historical Society and Museum, Connecticut | 32
Princeton University Art Museum, New Jersey | 10
Storm King Art Center, New York (contemporary sculpture) | 27
Union Church in Pocantico Hills, New York (Chagall windows) | 19
Weir Farm, Connecticut | 35

Village Walks

Allaire State Park, New Jersey, an abandoned village | 01
Bedford Village, New York | 20
Cold Spring, New York, a Hudson River village | 21
Hope, New Jersey, a Moravian village | 09
Lambertville, New Jersey, a Delaware River village | 37
Litchfield, Connecticut, a colonial village | 32
New Hope, Pennsylvania | 38
Northport, New York, a Long Island village | 17
Nyack, New York, a riverfront village | 31
Ocean Grove, New Jersey, a Methodist village | 07
Southport, Connecticut, "Jewel of Long Island Sound" | 34
Spring Lake, New Jersey, a Jersey shore village | 01

Preserves and Sanctuaries

Bowman's Hill State Wildlife Preserve, Pennsylvania | 36 | 37
Brinton Brook Audubon Sanctuary, New York | 18
Caumsett State Park, Long Island | 13
Devil's Den, Connecticut | 47
Gedney Brook Sanctuary, New York | 45
Great Swamp National Wildlife Refuge, New Jersey | 42
Greenwich Audubon Center, Connecticut | 47
Jamaica Bay Wildlife Refuge, New York | 44
Larsen Sanctuary, Connecticut | 47

Walks through History

Major and Minor Birding Sites

If You Prefer a Guided Walk or Tour

Vanderbilt Museum, Long Island (historic estate/natural history;
    tour required) | 14
West Point Military Academy, New York (military site) | 27

Enjoying Fall Foliage

Applewood Orchards and Winery, New York | 30
Cold Spring, New York | 21
Croton, New York | 18
Hope, New Jersey | 09
Kaaterskill Falls, New York | 25
Litchfield, Connecticut | 32
Putnam Memorial State Park, Connecticut | 33
Rockefeller State Park Preserve, New York | 22
Storm King Art Center, New York | 27

Cold Weather and Off-Season Outings (Including Indoors)

Caumsett State Park, Long Island | 13
Doris Duke Gardens, New Jersey | 04
Mianus River Gorge Wildlife Refuge and Botanical Preserve, New York | 20
Nyack Beach State Park, New York | 31
Piermont, New York | 28
Planting Fields Arboretum, Long Island | 15
Princeton University, New Jersey | 10
Rockefeller State Park Preserve, New York | 22
Rockland Lake, New York | 26
Sagamore Hill, Long Island | 16
Sandy Hook, New Jersey | 40
Vanderbilt Museum, Long Island | 14

Fruits, Vegetables, Mushrooms, and Wine

Applewood Orchards and Winery, New York | 30
Bowman's Hill State Wildflower Preserve and Medicinal Trail,
    Pennsylvania | 36 | 37
Cheesequake State Park, New Jersey (mushroom hunting) | 03
Haight Vineyards and Winery, Connecticut | 32
Jenny Jump State Forest, New Jersey (mushroom hunting) | 03
Mianus River Gorge Wildlife Refuge and Botanical Preserve, New York
    (mushroom hunting) | 20
Nyack farmers' market, New York | 31

Nature Centers and Interpretative Trails

Famous Houses and Interesting Estates

Waterfronts, Waterfalls, and Seashores

Walks for the Fittest

Of Interest to Children

About the Authors

Marina Harrison and Lucy D. Rosenfeld are lifelong friends and walking companions. They have collaborated on eight guidebooks, including for The Globe Pequot Press, *Gardenwalks in New England, Garden Walks in the Mid-Atlantic States,* and *Gardenwalks in the Southeast;* and *Artwalks in New York* (New York University Press), and *A Guide to Green New Jersey: Nature Walks in the Garden State* (Rutgers University Press). Both enjoy discovering new places of natural beauty and historic and artistic interest.